SECRET RAMSGATE

Andy Bull

with photography by Nick Barham

Sincere thanks are due to Michael Child of Michael's Bookshop, No. 72 King Street, Ramsgate, for his sterling work in discovering and reprinting so many illuminating books about the town and its history.

First published 2019

Amberley Publishing
The Hill, Stroud
Gloucestershire, GL5 4EP

www.amberley-books.com

ISBN 978 1 4456 9255 5 (print)
ISBN 978 1 4456 9256 2 (ebook)

British Library Cataloguing in Publication Data.
A catalogue record for this book is available from the British Library.

Origination by Amberley Publishing.
Printed in Great Britain.

Contents

Preface

It is almost impossible to exaggerate the vital role Ramsgate has played in England's rich history, and yet the town's importance is often overlooked.

It is, after all, right by the spot where Caesar's invasion force came ashore, and where Napoleon sought to emulate him, but was dissuaded. It is also where St Augustine landed on his mission to establish Christianity in England.

In the nineteenth century, Ramsgate was one of the finest resorts in the land. As the numerous blue plaques that dot the town's elegant crescents and squares attest, the town was once frequented by kings and queens, nobility, prime ministers, and authors, artists, scientists and radicals of the utmost eminence. What of the stories behind those plaques, and those visits?

This book explores a Ramsgate that deserves to be much better known, revealing why, for example, the future Queen Victoria almost died here, and examining the crucial role of a Ramsgate doctor in saving her life.

We find out why eminent resident Augustus Welby Pugin, architect of the interiors of the Palace of Westminster, was called 'the devil incarnate' by a Ramsgate clergyman.

We look at why another resident, Sir Moses Montefiore, built a replica of Rachel's Tomb in Ramsgate, and exported a Ramsgate windmill to Jerusalem.

We explore the lives of Sir William Garrow, who first used the phrase 'innocent until proven guilty', and laid the foundation for our modern legal system, and of Mary Townley, one of the first female architects, who created many of the finest buildings in Ramsgate.

We relish all the colour of a town in which Caroline, estranged wife of George IV, allegedly dallied with a naval officer; where the abandoned wife of a previous Duke of Sussex sought refuge; Jane Austen set scenes of seduction; Charles Dickens thrilled at the sight of a lady lion tamer; and Karl Marx and Joseph Engels complained about the *petit bourgeoisie* flooding in on cheap rail tickets.

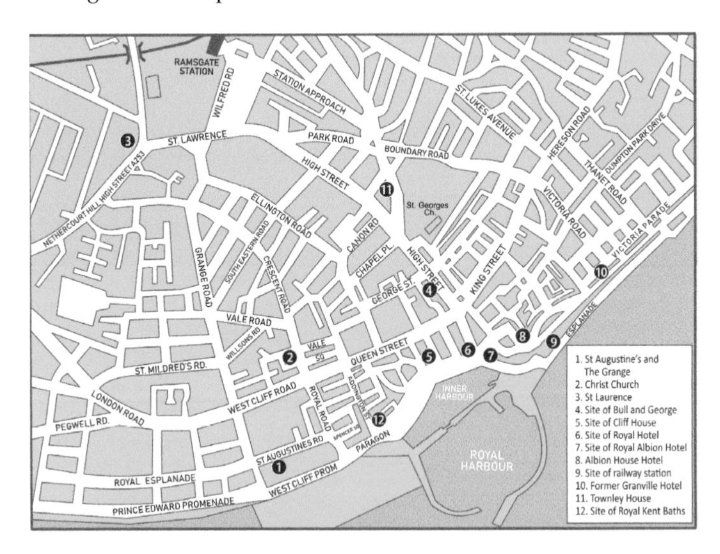

1. Ebbsfeet's Four Starring Roles in British History

Today Ebbsfleet is an easily overlooked place. The name survives in a lane and farmhouse 1.5 miles south of Cliffs End, just off the Sandwich Road. Yet Ebbsfleet has been a place of huge significance at four points in British history, one only recently confirmed.

Caesar, 54 BC

In 1724 Daniel Defoe cast an aspersion on Ramsgate that was not finally refuted until 2017. In his *A Tour Thro' the Whole Island of Great Britain,* the novelist and journalist best known for *Robinson Crusoe* described Ramsgate as:

> ...a small port, [where] the inhabitants are mighty fond of having us call it Roman's-Gate; pretending that the Romans under Julius Caesar made their first attempt to land here, when he was driven back by a storm; but soon returned, and coming on shore, with a good body of troops beat back the Britons, and fortify'd his camp, just at the entrance of the creek, where the town now stands; all which may be true for ought any one knows, but is not to be prov'd, either by them or anyone else; and is of so little concern to us, that it matters nothing whether here or at Deal, where others pretend it was.

Julius Caesar. (The Wellcome Collection)

Pegwell Bay, where Caesar's fleet landed in 54 BC.

Ebbsfleet, a little place with a huge role in English history. (Nick Barham)

In 2017, archaeologists from the University of Leicester proved the people of Ramsgate right and Defoe wrong when they discovered the exact place at Ebbsfleet, beside Pegwell Bay, where Caesar's fleet landed at noon on 5 July 54 BC. The site was on farmland, on a spit of higher ground that, in the first century, jutted out into the Wantsum Channel, which then divided the Isle of Thanet from mainland Kent.

It was a discovery that Andrew Fitzpatrick, research associate at the University of Leicester, says disproves the long-held theory that Caesar landed at Walmer, 15 miles to the south, and one which changes history.

In a series of surveys and excavations from 2015 to 2017 the Leicester archaeologists discovered Caesar's base: a 20-hectare (50-acre) enclosure, defended by ditches 2 metres deep and 5 metres wide, which were carbon dated to the first century. The iron tip of a Roman spear or pilum was found at the bottom of the ditch. The site likely contained a fort, and served to protect the invaders from attack.

It is known that Caesar came to Britain twice, first in 55 BC – unsuccessfully – then a year later, and that his British campaign followed his decisive victory in the battle for Gaul. Similar weapons and identical defensive ditches have been found at the site of that battle.

Fitzpatrick says the landscape at his excavation site, beside the large sandy beach with chalk cliffs to the east, matches Caesar's own description, in *The Gallic War,* of 'a sandy open shore' where his 800 ships found a safe anchorage and where his 20,000 troops and 2,000 horses could be landed in a day. This, says Fitzpatrick, is 'a perfect description of Pegwell Bay', the only bay on the east coast of Kent with an open sandy shore large enough to accommodate such a vast fleet.

However, not all went entirely to plan. The fleet was buffeted by a fierce storm, and many ships broke anchor, smashing against each other and causing damage that, Caesar wrote, took thousands of shipwrights to repair.

Fitzpatrick says the finds at Ebbsfleet also raise doubts over the long-held belief that Caesar's two campaigns had little lasting impact on Britain, with the invasion by Claudius in AD 43 being far more important. In fact, it may well be that although Caesar returned to France after both his incursions and left no garrison here, he laid the ground for the strong alliances with the kings of south-east England that were evidently in place by 20 BC.

By Caesar's account, he established a peace accord with them in 54 BC, sending hostages from ruling families back to Rome to ensure the treaties were adhered to. In this way, Caesar may well have bequeathed Claudius a relatively easy military victory in AD 43, and an occupation that endured until the fifth century.

DID YOU KNOW?

A curious relic of the Roman presence in Ramsgate was uncovered in the 1880s when James Hillier found a 3-foot-long horn from a white rhinoceros during excavations on the East Cliff, close to the Granville Hotel. At first it was believed to be a whale bone. An account in *Archaeologia Cantiana* suggested: 'The Romans may have introduced the living animal for the arena, or the horn may have been used for detecting poison in the cup, as the Romans and Greeks believed in the efficacy of its shavings for such detection.'

Hengest and Horsa, 449

Hengest and Horsa were warrior brothers, mercenaries who came to Kent from Germany, landing at Ebbsfleet in 449. They came to fight for Vortigern, King of the Britons, against

Scots and Picts encroaching from the north. Vortigern's forces triumphed, but Hengest and Horsa, unimpressed by what they considered the worthless Britons and covetous of their rich land, gathered a force from their homeland and defeated him.

The Venerable Bede's eighth-century *Ecclesiastical History of the English People* relates that Horsa was killed in battle in 455, but Hengist became king of Kent, reigning until his death in 488. Saxons, Angles and Jutes came to the conquered land, the Jutes settling in Kent, the Saxons in Sussex, Wessex and Essex, and the Angles in East Anglia, Northumbria and Mercia.

Some scholars see Hengist and Horsa as mythical but others, including J. R. R. Tolkien, author of *Lord of the Rings*, believe they are historical figures. Hengist's symbol, a prancing white horse, has been retained down the ages, and appears on the coat of arms of Kent.

St Augustine, 597

On Cottington Road, just to the west of Cliffs End, a Celtic stone cross stands behind a fence. This is St Augustine's Cross, erected in 1884 to mark the spot at which Augustine, sent from Rome to establish Christianity in England, met the Kentish king, Ethelbert, on his landing at Ebbsfleet.

DID YOU KNOW?

In 1969, a hoverport was built at Pegwell Bay, from which hovercraft could transport thirty cars and 250 passengers across to Calais in as little as twenty-two minutes. The service, operated by Hoverlloyd, became uneconomic when the price of oil rocketed in the 1970s, and ceased in 1982. The buildings were demolished and the site abandoned.

Christianity was a minority faith at the time of the Romans, and almost disappeared after their departure. Augustine needed to convert the king before the people of Kent would follow. He did so, baptising him, it is believed, on Whit Sunday 597.

The cross, commissioned by Earl Granville, Foreign Secretary, was erected at the spot where a tree called St Augustine's oak had stood until the nineteenth century. The baptism is believed to have taken place at a nearby stream, called St Augustine's Well. The cross is sited in Cottmanfield, whose original meaning was 'field of the man of God'.

According to the *Catholic Enclyclopedia*:

> Ethelbert was originally very suspicious of Augustine as he was brought up to believe priests practised magic. Rumour had it that Augustine could make tails grow on the backs of those who displeased him. Ethelbert met the tall Roman abbot in the open air rather than under cover to protect himself against the abbot's magic. The king listened patiently to the abbot's sermon and promised the monks shelter and protection at Canterbury. He considered the claims of the Catholic missionary for a time before converting.

St Augustine's Cross.
(Nick Barham)

St Augustine baptising Ethelbert,
from a fourteenth-century
illuminated manuscript.

By the end of the year, Augustine had 10,000 converts and went on to become the first Archbishop of Canterbury, though the title came later. The saint's connections with Ramsgate were revived in 2012 when St Augustine's Church, built by the Victorian architect Augustus Welby Pugin, became St Augustine's National Shrine. We will explore that story in chapter 6.

St Mildred, 680s

The final towering figure to land at Ebbsfleet was a young woman who would later become St Mildred, patron saint of Thanet, and who has given her name to St Mildred's Bay and many other Kent locations. Mildred, or Mildrith as her name was spelled at the time, became abbess of Minster Abbey, and was made a saint after her death. Her story is a compelling one.

As a young girl, Mildred, born around 660 and the granddaughter of King Ethelbert of Kent, was sent to be educated at the convent of Chelles, near Paris, by her mother, who was the then abbess at Minster.

At Chelles, a young nobleman made Mildred an offer of marriage. Mildred was very beautiful, being described by the chronicler Goscelin as 'the fairest lily of the English'. She rejected the nobleman, but the abbess of Chelles, Wilcoma, who was related to him, was determined the marriage should take place. When Mildred would not respond to persuasion she used threats and violence against her. Mildred fled, pursued by armed men across France.

St Mildred in a modern icon by Peter Murphy. (Peter Murphy – www.petermurphyicons.co.uk)

St Mildred's Priory, Minster. (Nick Barham)

The legend of her escape is remembered in the village of Millam, in Flanders, where Mildred was given shelter. A chapel, built in her honour, still stands on the edge of woodland where she hid, waiting for a chance to sail across the channel to Thanet.

Her ship anchored off Ebbsfleet and Mildred, anxious to get ashore as soon as possible, stepped from it onto a large rock that, legend had it, retained the imprint of her foot. She took refuge at Minster Abbey.

DID YOU KNOW?
Ramsgate once set its clocks five minutes and forty-one seconds ahead of Greenwich Mean Time. Ramsgate Mean Time was commonly used by south coast seafarers, who would set their chronometers by the time shown on the clock on the harbourside Clock House tower. In 1840 Greenwich became the new accepted standard, as the sign on the Clock House makes clear.

The story of Mildred's ill use and dramatic escape proved a powerful one, and Ebbsfleet became a place of pilgrimage to the extent that veneration of Mildred eclipsed even that afforded to St Augustine. The legend developed that powder from what became known as St Mildred's Rock could bring about miraculous cures, which led to the rock being dug up and transferred to Minster Abbey.

Ramsgate once set its clocks five minutes and forty-one seconds ahead of Greenwich Mean Time.

Mildred was attracting so many pilgrims to Minster that, in 1033, it was decided by the Abbot of St Augustine's Abbey, Canterbury, to dedicate a shrine to her there, and transfer her remains to it. According to the *Life of Mildred* her removal was intended to be carried out in secret, but

> The people of Thanet, happening to hear of the monks' doings, gave chase ... arming themselves with swords and staves and weapons of all sorts, to recover the body of their glorious Saint. But the monks had a fair start; and when the angry multitude first sighted them, they had already secured the ferry boats at Sarre, and were rowing swiftly over the broad waters of the Wantsum.

St Mildred's memory lives on. There is an Anglo-Saxon church dedicated to her at Canterbury, built around the time her shrine was dedicated. Public veneration of St Mildred has continued since the eighth century at Chelles and Millam, the two sites associated with her in France. It was interrupted in England following the Reformation, but was revived at Minster after a break of three centuries.

The former abbey there had become a private house, but a small group of Benedictine nuns from Bavaria bought it in 1937 and established St Mildred's Priory. A relic of St Mildred (a fragment of bone) was brought here from Holland in 1953, and enshrined at the priory.

2. Ramsgate Harbour and the Goodwin Sands

Ramsgate owes its existence to a storm, or rather two storms. In 1703, the English fleet was hoping to ride out a terrible hurricane, along with a great number of merchant ships, in the Downs, an area of relatively sheltered sea between the Goodwin Sands and the Kent coast. With no sizeable harbour to head to, they were at the mercy of the elements, and the elements showed no mercy. At least thirteen warships, forty merchant vessels and 2,168 lives were lost.

Clearly, a safe harbour needed to be built near the Downs. The obvious place was at Sandwich, 6 miles west of Ramsgate. Sandwich was a well-established Cinque Port, part of that rich and prosperous confederation including Dover, New Romney, Hythe and Hastings. In return for allowing their ships and sailors to be used by the Crown, the Cinque Ports enjoyed significant trade concessions and the right to run their own affairs.

Ramsgate barely existed. The closest village was St Lawrence, 1.5 miles inland. Ramsgate itself was a mere fishing hamlet with a small pier or breakwater offering precious little protection in a storm.

The great storm of 1703.

Ramsgate Harbour early in the last century.

Ramsgate Harbour today, at high tide with open access to the inner marina.

For forty-five years, the politicians prevaricated. No harbour was built. So when, in 1748, another great storm struck, the only hope for ships was to try for that tiny harbour at Ramsgate. Numerous vessels sought sanctuary there, several sank, scores were damaged, and many lives were lost. The wooden pier, which dated from the time of Henry VIII, was torn to pieces.

In the wake of this second – avoidable – tragedy, construction began on a new harbour, but not at Sandwich. In the intervening half century, its harbour had begun to silt up, an extension of the process that had seen the Wantsum Channel, which in Roman times divided Thanet from the mainland of Kent, reduced to a mere trickle. When seamen were consulted, they said that Ramsgate was the obvious place to build. If, in a storm, their anchors could not hold them on the Downs and they had to set sail, the prevailing winds would drive them directly to Ramsgate. Parliament concurred.

Ramsgate's future importance was assured. Its 46-acre harbour, sheltering in the protective arms of its stone east and west piers, would make it the only substantial port between Portsmouth and London, Dover not being developed until the nineteenth century.

The Civil Engineer and Architects' Journal reported that what had been a mere creek where only twenty-nine vessels called in a typical year before the completion of the harbour was, by 1848, receiving 1,606.

However, there were enormous problems along the way, all every bit as intractable as those that have dogged modern-day civil engineering projects such as the Channel Tunnel and Crossrail. By the 1770s, when Ramsgate Harbour was supposedly completed, it was virtually useless. So much sand had accumulated in it that at low tide this wasn't a deep-water basin: it was a beach!

A bust of John Smeaton. (Andy Mabbett under Creative Commons 3.0)

It would take two decades and a brilliant man to solve the problems. Step forward John Smeaton (1724–92), father of civil engineering, creator of the Eddystone Lighthouse and inventor of mortar that could set under water. His achievement was such that in 1791 he was asked to write *An Historical Report on Ramsgate Harbour,* a comprehensive account of the problems faced, and the solutions found.

The first challenge concerned the silting up of the new harbour. Smeaton wrote: 'There was not less than 268,000 cubic yards of silt in the harbour ... [and] the two barges then employed by the trustees, with ten men each, got about seventy tons of silt per day ... the harbour, at this rate, would be above twelve years in clearing, even supposing that no fresh silt was to come in during that time.'

With no river flowing into the harbour, there was nothing to flush out the sand brought in on each tide. Seaton proposed dividing the harbour in two by building a cross wall, thereby creating an inner harbour, fitted with sluices and a set of dock gates through which ships could pass. As the tide rose, these sluices would be opened so that the inner

Left: The entrance to the inner basin or marina.

Below: Boats in the outer marina. (Nick Barham)

Boats in the inner marina. (Nick Barham)

basin filled with water, but then kept closed as the tide ebbed. When this water was released it would flow through the outer harbour, clearing the silt.

The idea worked. However, the cross wall caused difficulty, experienced at high tide. As the water flowed in, 'the harbour had been greatly agitated, and at some particular times rather unsafe for ships to lie in, which was not the case before building the cross wall'. The reason was that 'the cross wall stopping and repelling the swell, it returns on account of its not having any vent or outlet, and causes that great disturbance and agitation now complained of'.

A further problem was the difficulty of approaching the harbour in rough weather:

> It was found that during all the time of full sea, a strong current sets almost right across the harbour's mouth; that is from west to east ... if, therefore, a vessel coming from the south, that is from the Downs, was to attempt to run into the harbour right across the current, it would carry her eastward thereof, so as to miss the entrance.

Smeaton came up with one solution that would solve both these problems. In 1788–89, an additional protective wall, or advanced pier, was built on to the end of the east pier. This sheltered the harbour mouth, 'meaning that a rough sea could no longer surge straight into it, and [this would] not only keep out the heavy sea that now tumbles in with hard gales of wind, and make the harbour more safe and more quiet, but that the coming into the harbour would in reality be more safe and easy'.

DID YOU KNOW?
The pressurised diving bell was first used by John Smeaton, its inventor, when building the East Pier at Ramsgate harbour. This airtight chamber could be lowered to the sea bed and air pumped in, enabling work to be done beneath the water level.

Finally, Smeaton was able to declare:

> Ramsgate harbour now exceeds the hopes ever entertained [for it] ... the harbour is of great importance to commercial navigation ... [and] has already been the means of saving property to the amount of between three and four million sterling, and between eight and nine thousand valuable lives.

Smeaton's solutions are still effective today, but they do make the harbour rather high maintenance. The great, 30-ton dock gates, which give access to the inner marina, must be opened two hours before each high tide, and closed two hours after it. This causes wear and tear and, in 2018, £750,000 was spent on repairs to them and the lifting bridge, which, when the gates are closed, allows people and vehicles to cross and, when opened, lets tall ships enter and leave the inner marina.

The calm harbour after Seaton's improvements.

The Goodwin Sands and the Mysterious Island of Lomea

The Goodwin Sands have long been a place of myth, mystery and dread. This 10-mile-long sandbank, 5 miles from Ramsgate Harbour, is notoriously dangerous to shipping.

At high tide the Goodwins are obscured, at low tide they rise half a metre above the waves, and shift position according to the tides and currents. At one time, five light ships and three coastal lighthouses warned mariners of their peril, yet over 2,000 ships are estimated to have perished on them. Today, just the East Goodwin Lightship and North Foreland Lighthouse remain to alert ships navigating the constantly busy Straits of Dover.

However, the Goodwins also serve a useful purpose. They create a breakwater to the anchorage in the Downs. Without the sands, the Downs would be impassable in easterly storms.

Excavations in 1817 by Trinity House to determine the feasibility of building a lighthouse on the Goodwins found, beneath 15 feet of sand, a stratum of London Clay above a bed of chalk. This led the geologist Charles Lyell to conclude that the Goodwins were not a mere sandbank, created by the currents and tides in the English Channel, but the remains of dry land, and once an island similar to the Isle of Sheppey.

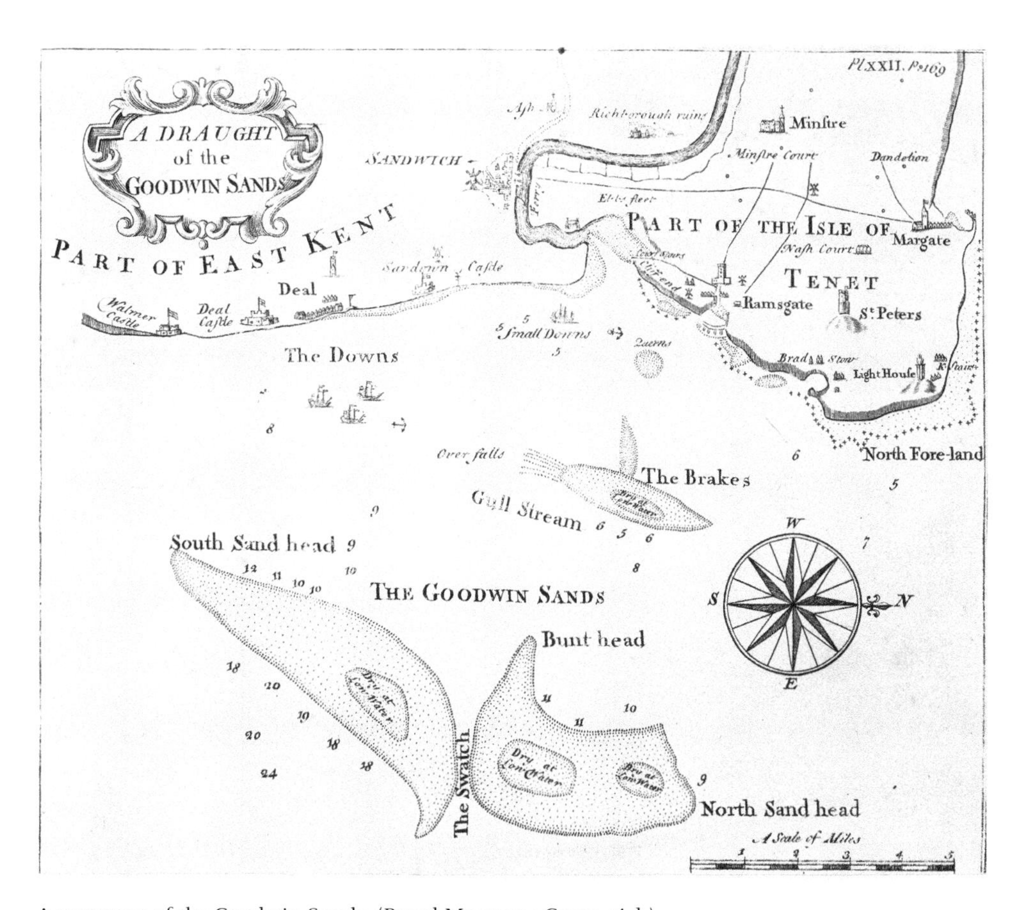

A 1750 map of the Goodwin Sands. (Royal Museums Greenwich)

East Goodwin Lightship while under repair at Harwich. (Eva Kröcher under GNU Free Documentation License 1.2)

The discovery, it was claimed by G. B. Gattie, a civil servant and historian, supported legends of a mysterious island, known to the Romans as Infera Insula or Lomea, Low Island, which had been overcome by the sea in 1099.

DID YOU KNOW?
On Jacob's Ladder, the stone staircase between Royal Parade and the harbour, there is an unusual feature. In the corners on each landing are curved stones designed as urine deflectors to deter would-be offenders. Anyone taking a pee would wet their feet! The steps are named after Jacob Stead, who built a set of wooden steps in 1754. This replacement stone structure dates from 1826.

A urine deflector, designed to deter Jacob's Ladder being used as a loo.

In his 1904 book *Memorials of the Goodwin Sands and Their Surroundings, Legendary and Historical* Gattie writes:

> Some of the early writers, in describing this coast, distinctly mention three islands ... one on the north, called *Tanatus* (Thanet) or *Teneth*, from the fire beacon on its heights; one on the south called *Eutupiae* or *Ruochini Insula* (Richborough); and one bearing south-east called *Infera Insula* (Lomea, or Low Island).

Therefore, Gattie goes on:

> As the Isle of Thanet is nearly surrounded by high cliffs, and as *Eutupiae* (Richborough) is now part of the mainland, it is evident that Lomea, the island lying to the south-east, and occupying the exact position of the present Goodwin Sands, must have been, as stated by the old writers, none other than the sea-girt island said to have formed part of the vast possessions, if not the actual home, of the great English statesman and warrior, the famous Earl Godwine, [Godwin].

Gattie explores the many myths about Lomea, and the supposed connection with Godwin. Godwin of Wessex (*c.* 1001–53) was one of the most powerful earls in England, whose daughter Edith married Edward the Confessor, and whose son Harold Godwinson, the last Anglo-Saxon king of England, was killed by William the Conqueror at the Battle of Hastings.

Hugh Latimer, preaching about the Goodwin Sands before Edward VI. (The Wellcome Collection)

Several legends are associated with the steeple of St Mildred's Church at Tenterden in the Weald of Kent, which, at the time, was a seaport.

One version is that Godwin, on one of his many military expeditions, penetrated the Weald and burned the palace of the king of Kent. Finding himself in peril from superior forces, says Gattie, 'he made a vow to the Blessed Virgin that should he return in safety to his island estate of Lomea, he would erect a steeple to the church at Tenterden in honour of the saints.' He was spared, but forgot his vow. The destruction of Lomea was the vengeance of Heaven.

Another version, which shows that the Tenterden/Lomea story was still being recounted in the fifteenth century, features the unexpected figures of Sir Thomas More and Hugh Latimer, Bishop of Worcester.

Latimer used it in a sermon preached before Edward VI, says Gattie, 'as a sort of parable ... against hasty and utterly illogical conclusions ... the Bishop, apparently, having been improperly accused of assisting the cause of rebellion by his eloquent preaching.'

In his sermon, Latimer recounted the story that Sir Thomas More was once sent to Kent to discover the cause of Goodwin's Sands, and the silting up of Sandwich's harbour. Among those he questioned was a 100-year-old man, who told him the story of Tenterden's steeple.

However, Latimer clearly thought the tale nonsense, and presumably was confident the king would concur, because he ended his sermon by saying: 'And even so, to my purpose, is preaching of God's Worde the cause of rebellion, as Tenterden steeple is a cause that Sandwich haven is decayed.'

Hovellers and Lifeboatmen

The trustees of Ramsgate harbour first established a lifeboat station in 1802, but there was a break in provision from 1824 to 1851. From 1865 the Royal National Lifeboat Institution took over. There were also unlicensed boats supplying ships in the Downs, offering pilotage through the Goodwins, mounting rescues when ships got into trouble and salvaging valuable cargoes.

In Ramsgate and elsewhere in Kent these men were known as hovellers, and were sometimes in competition with the Ramsgate lifeboat as to who could reach a stricken vessel first. Gattie has this to say of them:

> The war of the elements is to them the opportunity of gain; and the greater and more terrible the storm, the greater and more likely their chances of a 'good hovel'... Eager eyes notice the deepening gloom and the rising gale, and when the storm fairly bursts in all its fury, when the breakers are rolling on the Sands and dashing with intense violence on the beach, then these brave fellows, fearing neither winds nor waves, quickly man one or other of their finely built luggers, rigged with a huge lug sail, and steer direct for the Goodwins, about the very last place that anyone would willingly seek during the prevalence of a heavy gale!

Ramsgate's lifeboat attending a ship in distress on the Goodwin Sands.

The "Aid" towing out smacks, Ramsgate

The tug *Aid 3* towing fishing smacks out of Ramsgate Harbour in 1906.

The Hovelling Boat Inn in York Street recalls Ramsgate's brave – and sometimes opportunistic – seafarers.

Rescues were dramatic, and perilous. Gattie writes that when the hovellers reached a wreck,

> The sail of the boat is lowered and the anchor dropped considerably to windward of the labouring ship ... the cable is then paid out yard by yard and the heavy rolling sea is allowed to carry the boat little by little towards the vessel till she is almost alongside. And now not a second is to be lost, and those of the ship's crew who are able to do so instantly leap into the boat; for if another wave catches her in this position she must be dashed to pieces. Then indeed is a moment of intense anxiety and peril, and all hands haul upon the cable with might and main for dear life until the boat gradually draws away from the wreck.

With so much money to be made from hovelling, salvage became very competitive. From 1843, steam tugs came into use at Ramsgate. They were kept with crew on board and steam up, ready to put to sea instantly. Their great advantage over the Ramsgate lifeboat, which was powered by oar and sail, was that tugs could get out of the harbour in the roughest conditions and, when they reached a stricken ship, could tow it out of danger.

Tugs including *Samson* and successors including *Aid*, which came into service in 1855, would work with the lifeboat, assisting in the rescue. The tug would tow the lifeboat out to the sands, upwind of the wreck, from where it could cross the shallow waters to take off survivors, while the tug steamed round in deep waters downwind to pick up any sailors who might have been washed there from the ship. *Aid* was followed by *Aid 2* and *Aid 3*.

Modern Plans for the Goodwin Sands

Over the past twenty years, several ambitious plans have been put forward that would have transformed the Goodwin Sands into a modern transport hub. The first, in 1968, was a Ministry of Transport scheme to reclaim them and construct a deep-water port. The second, in 1985, was to create a two-runway airport on three reclaimed islands. Such an airport would have had twenty-four-hour take-off and landing, there being no local residents to disturb. In 2012 the engineering firm Beckett Rankine expanded on the airport idea, proposing five runways and arguing that placing an airport here offered the most sustainable option for expanding runway capacity in the South East, because the sands have no environmental protection, and no flights need take place over populated areas.

DID YOU KNOW?

In 2013, a German bomber was dug out from beneath Goodwin Sands. It had made an emergency landing there after a raid on Ramsgate in August 1940, and become buried. When the Dornier Do 17 crashed, two of its four-man crew were killed on impact, with the others taken prisoner. The plane, one of two surviving craft of its type, is being painstakingly restored at the RAF museum at Hendon in North London.

DID YOU KNOW?

William Shakespeare mentions the Goodwin Sands in *The Merchant of Venice*, writing: 'Antonio hath a ship of rich lading wrecked on the narrow seas; the Goodwins, I think they call the place; a very dangerous flat and fatal, where the carcasses of many a tall ship lie buried.'

In *Moby Dick*, Herman Melville writes: 'the dead of mankind ... tell no tales, though containing more secrets than the Goodwin Sands.'

3. Ramsgate at War

The Napoleonic Wars

Like Caesar before him, Napoleon planned to land his invasion force at Pegwell Bay. He never made it, but the Napoleonic Wars transformed Ramsgate. The new harbour was the main embarkation point for troops headed across the Channel. Barracks were thrown up on East and West Cliffs, and fine housing built for officers.

No trace now remains of the barracks, stables, parade grounds and gun batteries, but the Napoleonic Wars (1803–15) are remembered in street names. Nelson Crescent, on West Cliff, honours Lord Nelson, who in 1805 defeated the French and Spanish at the Battle of Trafalgar, but tragically died. On East Cliff, Wellington Crescent and Plains of Waterloo honour, respectively, the man who finally defeated the French at the Battle of Waterloo, in June 1815, and the land on which the battle was fought.

Much of the war was run from Ramsgate. George Elphinstone, Admiral Lord Keith, who was overall commander of the North Sea and Channel fleets, had his home and headquarters here at East Cliff Lodge. Wellington, at the time Major-General Sir Arthur Wellesley, lived at No. 1 Chatham Place, and his officers lodged at the London Hotel, where the HSBC bank now stands in the High Street. Later, in 1812–13, when his brother the Marquis of Wellesley had replaced Lord Keith at East Cliff Lodge, Wellington stayed there.

Lord Nelson.

Nelson Crescent.
(Nick Barham)

Over 300 ships took 50,000 men, horses and supplies to the Continent. In 1815, thirty-four ships look the Household Cavalry and Royal Dragoons to Ostend to join Wellington and play a crucial role in his victory at the Battle of Waterloo. Many of the wounded who made it back to Ramsgate are buried in St Laurence's churchyard.

Even with its harbour now working perfectly, Ramsgate struggled to cope with the enormous traffic. As Robert K. Sutcliffe writes, in *British Expeditionary Warfare and the Defeat of Napoleon, 1793–1815*:

> there was insufficient space ... and too few moorings for all the necessary troop ships, victuallers, store ships and naval vessels. Once loaded, transports had to be moved on to allow others into the harbour. They gathered in huge numbers ... in the Downs to await the embarkation of the whole force, the loading of the supply ships and finally the arrival of the naval escort. It was not unusual for those ships loaded early in the process to ... be at anchor for four to six weeks before commencing their voyage.

One of the well-known facets of the other great Napoleonic hero – Horatio, Lord Nelson – is his affair with Emma, Lady Hamilton. Far less well known is the small but significant part Ramsgate played in their lives.

Born Amy Lyon, the daughter of a Cheshire blacksmith, she travelled alone to London at the age of twelve, changing her name to Emma Hart. She found work in the theatre before becoming muse to the famous society portraitist George Romney. Romney's many paintings, and her beauty, made Emma one of London's greatest celebrities. She had affairs with various titled men before, at twenty-one, marrying Sir William Hamilton, aged fifty-five, and becoming Lady Hamilton.

When she met Nelson he was a great war hero, and a married man, but was dangerously sick. She nursed him, they fell in love and secretly had a daughter, Horatia. Emma lived openly with Nelson and Sir William in a *ménage à trois*. The popular press became obsessed with Emma. Any little detail was newsworthy: her dress, how she decorated her home, her dinner party menus etc.

The Duke of Wellington. (The Wellcome Collection)

Wellington Crescent. (Nick Barham)

Above left: The Duke of Wellington's house, No. 1 Chatham Place.

Above right: Emma, Lady Hamilton, Nelson's mistress. (The Wellcome Collection)

In 1802, with Sir William finding it all a bit much, Emma tried to please her husband by holidaying with him in Ramsgate. Reporters followed their every move, and pestered her friends for titbits about her.

As Kate Williams writes in *England's Mistress*, 'everywhere she went she was pursued by the press and besieged by crowds, people hunting for a favour, and crazed obsessives, greedy to touch the star's mantle'. The *Morning Herald* reported on her swimming, saying 'a lady swimmer at Ramsgate ... is now the morning gaze of the place', and that, as such an excellent swimmer, she was 'secure against any *marine enemy,* but as she is young and beautiful, she is perhaps more in danger from the *land sharks*'. One of those land sharks was the Prince of Wales, the future George IV. His infatuation, and the attention he lavished on Emma, sent Nelson into a jealous fury.

While in Ramsgate, Emma had arranged for her daughter Horatia, whom she and Nelson claimed was their godchild, to be taken to nearby Margate, where she could meet her in secret. On the first attempt Emma forgot the address where they were to meet, and was terrified at what Nelson would think of her as a mother should he find out.

Meanwhile, writes Kate Williams, Sir William was 'miserable in the bustle of bathers and fashion [and] wished he were alone with her'. Emma was exasperated. It took all her effort to dodge the press and meet her daughter, she didn't have time for his complaining.

He threatened her with separation, saying 'I have but a very little time to live, and every moment is precious to me.'

He died in Emma's arms in April 1804, with Nelson holding his hand. Nelson was soon back at war, as commander-in-chief of the Mediterranean fleet, and Emma was left alone. She begged him to allow her to come and live with him on his ship, but he told her it was impossible. In 1804 she was back in Ramsgate, now cutting a sad and lonely figure. She had become pregnant before Nelson left, but the little girl survived only six weeks. Now forty, with her fertility declining, Emma was terrified she would lose Nelson if she were unable to give him the large family he craved. So she came to swim and drink seawater, which was believed to improve fertility, in the hope she might fall pregnant swiftly once her lover returned.

It was not to be. Emma and Nelson met just once more before his death at the Battle of Trafalgar in 1805.

While Nelson and Wellington were responsible for the two historic victories of the Napoleonic Wars, Ramsgate can also boast the great forgotten hero of the conflict. For it was Admiral Lord Keith, who, as commander-in-chief of the North Sea, successfully defended the home shores.

As Kevin D. McCranie writes in *Admiral Lord Keith and the Naval War against Napoleon*, the command of the North Sea squadron was vital between 1803 and 1806. With 200 frigates and other small warships under his command, the largest squadron in the Royal Navy, Keith's role was to prevent Napoleon's invasion force landing at Pegwell Bay, which was considered imminent. Rather than serve afloat like other admirals, Keith masterminded his far quieter but no less vital victory from East Cliff Lodge, a house that we will hear a great deal more about in subsequent chapters.

First World War: the First Zeppelin Raid

Thanet suffered 119 bombing raids during the First World War, and Ramsgate bore the brunt, becoming the most raided town in England. The first Zeppelin raid came in the early hours of Monday 17 May 1915, when Zeppelin LZ38, flying high and looking no bigger than a cigar, dropped twenty bombs on the town, sixteen of them incendiaries, which burst into flames upon impact, and four packed with high explosives.

One of the latter crashed through the Bull and George Hotel at No. 14 High Street. Photographs taken at the scene in the morning show the clock on the front wall stopped at 1.47, the point the bombs exploded.

The *Illustrated London News* reported:

> Two guests staying in the hotel, Mr and Mrs John Smith, of Thornton Heath, [Surrey] were precipitated into the cellar amid falling debris, and were seriously injured. A barmaid, Miss Kate Moffatt, was roused just in time by the assistant housekeeper, Miss Pilkington, and had a wonderful escape. Just as she left her room a bomb crashed through it.
>
> 'We were on the fourth floor,' said Miss Pilkington. 'We rushed down the corridor and got into the yard. All the bedrooms in the front are gone, and with them the coffee-room and the commercial room. The bomb passed clean through Mr and Mrs Smith's bedroom, and carried them into the cellar, where they were found by the police.'

The Bull & George after the Zeppelin raid of 17 May 1915 in which a couple died.

Chief Inspector Paine of the Ramsgate Borough Police would later recount that he found John Smith, forty-two, in the cellar, embedded up to his waist in rubble, and pinned down by a rafter that had fallen across his legs. Paine and others got him out through a hole blown in the pavement and he was taken to Ramsgate General Hospital.

His 'wife', Florence, was taken to a military hospital at Nethercourt House, suffering from broken ribs and severe shock. Despite his very serious injuries, John insisted on visiting her. He had to be helped into and out of the taxi that took him there.

The following evening, John died of heart failure brought on by severe shock. Florence followed him two days later. At their inquests, conducted by Ramsgate's coroner Dr F. W. Hardman, it became clear that John and Florence were not married, nor did they live together. In fact, she was Florence Lamont, forty-three, wife of Albert Lamont, and the address given for Mr and Mrs Smith, in Thornton Heath, Surrey, was her marital home. John Smith had lived 6 miles away, in Sutton. In what was described as 'Husband's Evidence' Albert Lamont, a clerk at the War Office, identified the body as that of his wife.

DID YOU KNOW?

In May 1917, the men of Torpedo Boat 4, moored in Ramsgate Royal Harbour, were at breakfast when one of their torpedoes exploded. Fourteen were killed and the boat sunk in an explosion that blew out windows on West Cliff and Harbour Parade and damaged 400 houses. Pockmarked brickwork can still be seen on buildings in Military Road.

It would seem that John, possibly a publican, and Florence, who worked like her husband at the War Office, had stolen a few days away together in Ramsgate. Until Saturday they had been staying on the seafront, in the Hotel St Cloud. John was born in Thanet, and perhaps wanted to show Florence the place in which he had grown up.

The coroner attributed John Smith's death to 'Wilful murder against the Kaiser' and Florence's to 'Death due to injuries received through an illegitimate and dastardly act of war.' The deliberate targeting of civilians was a previously unknown tactic of war, and led to German actions being referred to as the war on women and children. The coroner added that 'anyone who took the view that the dropping of bombs on the civilian population ... was a legitimate act of war, must be totally unacquainted with international law.'

The Bull and George had to be demolished, making it the first building destroyed by bombing in Ramsgate.

During the Napoleonic Wars, Wellington's troops had stabled their horses at the hotel, then known as the Bull Inn. In the Second World War the roof of Woolworth's, built on the site of the hotel, was used as an observation post for civilian members of the Royal Observation Corps, known as the fire watchers. Recently discovered pictures drawn on the walls of a stairwell in what is now Poundland, designed to help watchers spot and differentiate between German and British planes, feature a German Dornier Do 17 bomber and an RAF Wellington. The watchers were there to spot incendiaries so that resulting fires could be quickly dealt with.

Hotel St Cloud, now the Comfort Inn, where the Zeppelin victims had been staying. (Nick Barham)

First World War: Ramsgate's Saddest Day

It was a sunny spring afternoon on 19 March 1916 and a group of children were walking to St Luke's Church Sunday school with their teacher, newly married twenty-three-year-old Gertrude Bishop.

As they walked along St Luke's Avenue at around 2 p.m., a bomb dropped from a German seaplane scored a direct hit on a car being driven by forty-nine-year-old mechanic Harry Divers, causing the petrol tank to explode, hurling him into the air and killing him instantly.

Shrapnel from the bomb, and the car, killed four children instantly, and a fifth died the next day. A further ten were horribly injured. A girl of nine, Grace Ward, had to have her right arm amputated. Mrs Bishop died two days later. The tragic loss of so many young lives made this the saddest, most devastating day for the town.

The dead were James Saxby, aged four, his six-year-old sister Gladys, seven-year-old Francis Hardwick, Herbert Gibbons, nine, and Ernest Philpott, twelve.

Earnest Philpott's brother and two sisters were injured. Another brother, fifteen-year-old George, saved one of his sisters by pushing her to the ground and throwing his body over hers as the bomb fell, but received a serious shrapnel wound from which he never recovered. He died the following year. His family said: 'The Germans have another death to account for.'

Information gathered on the Lives of the First World War website details what a devasting blow this was for their families and for the town. A mass funeral was held the next Thursday at St Luke's, followed by burial at Ramsgate Cemetery. Many townspeople attended. On the hundredth anniversary of the tragedy, a commemorative service was held at St Luke's, followed by a procession to the cemetery, where the Saxby children's graves had been restored the previous year.

The grave of the Saxby children, victims of a 1916 bombing raid, in Ramsgate Cemetery. (Nick Barham)

Second World War: Ramsgate's Tunnels

It took three requests before the government would allow Ramsgate council to dig a network of deep tunnels giving shelter to 60,000.

The 3.5-mile network of tunnels, the most extensive underground protection network in the country, was the brainchild of the borough engineer, Dick Brimmell. As Nick Catford recounts in *The Ramsgate Tunnels*, the council first applied to the Home Office following Hitler's annexation of Austria in 1938, but were told the idea was premature. They tried again after the Munich Agreement, in which France said it would not assist Czechoslovakia if Germany occupied the Sudetenland. It wasn't until the spring of 1939, when Hitler invaded Czechoslovakia, that permission was granted and excavations began.

A key component was the former railway tunnel that ran from Dumpton Park for 0.75 miles beneath the town to come out on the beach. It had been dug in 1863 by the London, Chatham & Dover Railway, but the line had proved difficult to operate. In 1936 it had been converted into the World Scenic Railway, on which narrow-gauge trains, the carriages fitted with spotlights to illuminate tableaux on the tunnel walls, ran from the beach up to a new terminus at Hereson Road.

A tunnel was then dug, at up to 70 feet below the surface, in a semi-circle around the town centre, starting at the western end of the harbour, following Addison Street,

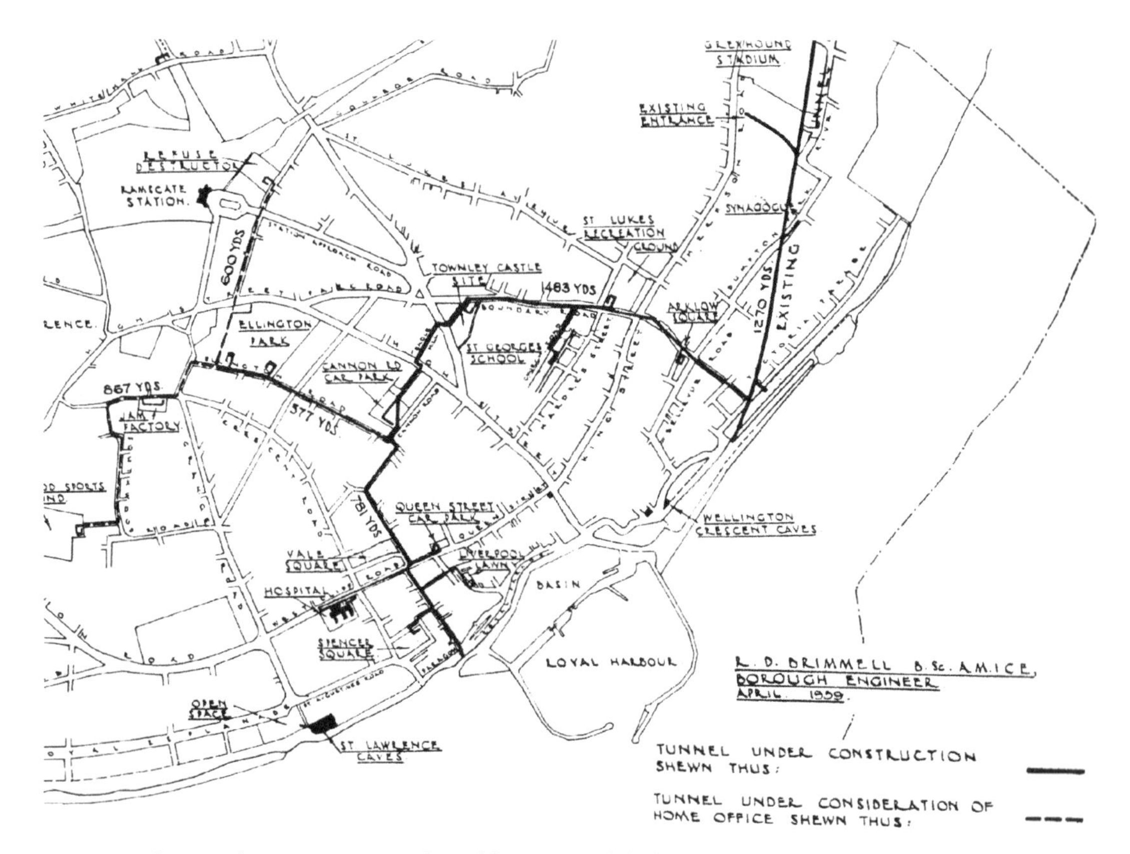

Map showing the extensive Second World War tunnel shelters dug beneath Ramsgate.

Britain's wartime leader Winston Churchill inspects bomb damage in Ramsgate, August 1940. (Imperial War Museum)

passing Vale Square as it ran along Marlborough Road, then swinging eastwards beneath parts of North Avenue and Cannon Road, crossing under the High Street, then beneath Eagle Road to Boundary Road and Victoria Road before joining the railway tunnel close to the beach.

A further tunnel, joining the main one beneath the junction of Canon Road and Ellington Road, ran up Ellington Road before splitting, one arm going under Ellington Park and Queens Gate Road to the railway station, the other under intervening streets to Southwood Road.

Ten spurs ran off the tunnel, one to the General Hospital in West Cliff Road, others to parks and open spaces, and there were fifteen other entrances around town, meaning no one was more than five minutes from safety in the event of an air raid. The network amounted to a complete underground city, and was highly effective in protecting the people of Ramsgate.

As each section was completed, those living close to it were allocated places. The tunnels were 6 feet high and 7 feet wide, with bench seating along the walls, chemical toilets in recesses each 80 feet and first aid posts every 1,000 feet. There were electric lights, with hurricane lamps in reserve, and a PA system playing wireless programmes and announcements. There was no smoking and no pets.

There were seats for 35,000, but up to 60,000 could be accommodated if necessary – adequate for the whole population of the town. The total cost for digging and fitting out the tunnels and converting the railway tunnel was £54,000 (£3.5 million at today's prices).

On the worst raid, on the afternoon of 24 August 1940, 500 bombs were dropped on Ramsgate in just half an hour, and while seventy-eight houses were destroyed and 1,200 damaged, the casualty rate of twenty-nine civilians and two soldiers dead plus fifty-nine people injured was remarkably light – thanks to the tunnels.

The main tunnel shelter, which formerly took the railway down to the sands.

DID YOU KNOW?
When, during the Second World War, a German mine-laying submarine was captured and blown up on the Goodwin Sands, one of its guns was saved and brought ashore, to be mounted as a souvenir on the West Cliff.

One victim of that devasting raid was eight-year-old Denis Rose. In *A Ramsgate Boy's Memories of the Second World War* he tells how he and his family were in the Anderson shelter in their garden at No. 60 Winstanley Crescent when a bomb blast lifted the shelter into the air then dumped it back on top of them, together with a pile of rubble. It took hours to dig them out, and they only avoided suffocation because they had been sheltering with their heads under a single bed.

Denis, his parents and sister Angela, five, moved in to the Boundary Road tunnel. He writes:

We lived in the tunnel for quite a long time while the council found us another place to live ... We had an alcove down there, it was about eight feet by six feet. We lived in that part and our two sets of bunk beds were opposite the main tunnel. We had Valor stoves to cook on and lived mainly on stews and potatoes.

My mother used to put me on the top bunk above my father, which was stupid really because, due to my bad nerves, I used to wet the bed. I remember every night getting punched out of bed from below and getting a good hiding for peeing on him...

They used to have dances down the big [former railway] tunnel ... They had a dance band, shops, canteen etc. Saturday was a big night and I used to walk from our alcove to the big tunnel (a mile or so) and watch the adults enjoying themselves ... they had a bar and everything. Even in the times of despair there were some highlights.

Second World War: Ramsgate and the Little Ships

One of Ramsgate's greatest contributions to the war effort was its role in Operation Dynamo, the successful evacuation of 338,226 troops from Dunkirk between 26 May and 4 June 1940. While Dover was the major centre for the Royal Navy, Ramsgate was the main hub for the 700 little ships, civilian craft including fishing boats, pleasure craft, paddle steamers and lifeboats that succeeded in bringing 43,000 safely home.

The little ships were vital at Dunkirk because many men had to be lifted from the gently shelving beaches, and only the little ships could get close enough to do so.

The little ship *Sundowner*, now restored and moored at Ramsgate.

Troops waiting to be rescued from the beach at Dunkirk.

Among the captains of the little ships was a man who had come through the most notorious disaster at sea. Commander Herbert Lightoller had survived the sinking of the *Titanic* in 1912. Lightoller had stayed on the ship until shortly before she went under, and was responsible for ensuring women and children got priority in the lifeboats launched from the *Titanic*'s port side. He stayed until all the lifeboats were launched and the ship was about to go under before diving into the sea and swimming to an upturned collapsible boat to which thirty were already clinging, and was rescued at dawn.

When the call came for Operation Dynamo, he insisted on taking his motor yacht, *Sundowner*, across the Channel himself, rather than handing it over to the navy. On the way over he rescued five men from the yacht *Westerly*, which had caught fire. Then he took *Sundowner* alongside a destroyer moored at the East Mole, one of two, mile-long stone and concrete breakwaters in Dunkirk harbour, and took off 122 troops. On the way home he was attacked by enemy aircraft, but used evasive techniques that were taught to him by his son, an RAF pilot, and made it back to Ramsgate. His actions inspired the character of Mr Dawson in Christopher Nolan's 2017 film *Dunkirk*.

Fast forward to 1986 and *Sundowner* was again in Ramsgate, sheltering from a storm that had caused her considerable damage. The then owners did not have the money to repair the boat, and were planning to cut her up with a chainsaw, when another veteran of the Dunkirk rescue recognised her as one of the little ships.

DID YOU KNOW?
Prime Minister Winston Churchill was visiting Ramsgate's bomb shelters when sirens announced a raid. The mayor was about to usher him into the Queen Street shelter when Winston lit one of his famous cigars. He had to be told that smoking was banned underground. Churchill said: 'There goes a good 'un', as he threw it to the ground.

John Knight was also sheltering from the storm, on *Fidelma*, another Operation Dynamo boat. Knight was a member of the Association of Dunkirk Little Ships and helped arrange for *Sundowner* to be restored, and the following year she became a permanent exhibit at Ramsgate's Maritime Museum. In 2012 she celebrated her hundredth birthday by taking part in the Thames Diamond Jubilee Pageant, celebrating the Queen's sixty years on the throne. Over 150 of the little ships have been identified and restored, and many take part in anniversary sailings from Ramsgate to Dunkirk.

The Ramsgate lifeboat *Prudential* was another of the little ships that answered the call, as John Grehan relates in *Dunkirk: Nine Days That Saved An Army*. The *Prudential's* coxswain Howard Primrose Knight and eight-man crew towed eight wherries – large, open rowing boats crewed by eighteen Royal Navy men – across the Channel. At Dunkirk, the wherries were able to go right up to the beach, taking men off, then row back to the *Prudential*, which could hold 160 men. Once full it would transfer the men to a larger ship in deeper water, then return and repeat the process. It took 800 men off the beaches. At night, on one of the trips to shore a voice called out 'I cannot see who you are. Are you a naval party?'

The response came: 'No sir, we are the men of the crew of the Ramsgate lifeboat.'

To which the voice called: 'Thank you, and thank God for such men as you have this night proved yourselves to be.'

Another Ramsgate-based little ship, a 56-foot passenger launch called the *New Britannic*, spent two days at Dunkirk, ferried 3,000 men to waiting ships and brought back a further eighty-three to Ramsgate. Skipper Walter Read was accompanied by his fifteen-year-old son Joe, believed to be the youngest to crew a little ship. After the war she worked as a pleasure boat in the West Country, but was decommissioned and almost scrapped. In 1996 she was restored and returned to Ramsgate, but is now at Conyer in Kent.

4. Royal Ramsgate

Above left: George IV granted Ramsgate Harbour its royal status. (Metropolitan Museum of Art)

Above right: Queen Caroline, spurned wife of George IV. (The Wellcome Collection)

Left: The obelisk erected in Ramsgate to thank George IV for favouring the town.

How Billy Biscuit Brought George IV to Ramsgate

How did Ramsgate's Royal Harbour get its regal status? The well-known answer is that the recently crowned George IV wished to acknowledge the fine send-off he received when he sailed from here in 1821 with the Royal Yacht Squadron to his other newly acquired dominion, the kingdom of Hanover.

The town returned the favour the following year when a 50-foot stone obelisk, modelled on two that stood at the entrance to ancient Thebes in Egypt, was erected alongside the harbour, thanking George for choosing Ramsgate.

However, there is much more to this mutual love-in than meets the eye. The reason George chose Ramsgate for his departure over Dover was highly political. To understand it, we have to go back a little, and consider the state of George IV's marriage to Caroline of Brunswick. The couple had been estranged since shortly after they wed in 1795.

Latterly, Caroline had been living in Italy with her lover Bartolomeo Bergami, while George was back with his long-term mistress Maria Fitzherbert.

When George's father, George III, died in 1820, and his son was to be crowned, Caroline decided to return and claim her rights as his queen. She came via Dover and, to the new king's fury, received a rapturous welcome from the people of that town. George banned Caroline from attending his coronation and, when she turned up anyway, had her repelled at bayonet point. She died a month later.

In light of Dover's disloyalty, the new king was highly receptive when Sir William Curtis, his great friend and Ramsgate resident, urged him to favour his town for departure to Hanover.

DID YOU KNOW?

The Royal Victoria Pavilion actually opened two years after the queen's death in 1903. It was designed by Stanley Davenport in the style of a Robert Adam orangery in just a week, and built in only six weeks.

Curtis was a fascinating character: a Cockney from Wapping whose family firm supplied ships biscuits to the Royal Navy, earning him the nickname Billy Biscuit. Curtis was ill-educated, uncouth, bulbous-nosed, obese, and a brilliant businessman. He made a fortune from shipping and banking.

Before setting sail, George stayed at Curtis's home, Cliff House, which stood on Cliff Street, where West Cliff Mansions is now. This was the finest residence among the grand terraces that now lined the seafront, and looked out to sea from atop the harbour's soaring rose-brick retaining wall.

Curtis and the king were widely ridiculed by the satirists of the day. Lord Byron, in 'Don Juan', wrote this of the pair:

> Tell them Sir William Curtis is a bore,
> Too dull even for the dullest of excesses,
> The witless Falstaff of a hoary Hal,
> A fool whose bells have ceased to ring at all.

Curtis, who was MP for the City of London, was mocked in the House of Commons, where he was credited with designating reading, writing and arithmetic 'The Three Rs'.

Nevertheless, Sir William was astute enough to cultivate the king, and bring glory to Ramsgate, as Terry Prue recounts in *King George IV, Power Politics and Ramsgate*. He organised a sumptuous feast and rapturous welcome before George IV's departure on 24 September, and on his return on 10 November.

For the king's arrival, Curtis arranged a welcome from thousands of townsfolk, who lined streets decorated with great floral displays, strewn with beach sand and illuminated with thousand of lights – as were the vessels in the harbour. That evening, at Cliff House, fourteen of the richest, most powerful men in the kingdom, including the Prime Minister, Lord Liverpool, enjoyed a feast that included soup made from a turtle brought to Ramsgate, live, aboard the *Eagle* steam packet. There followed a grand dress ball for 250 nobility and gentry in the Assembly Rooms in the Albion Hotel, which stood on the corner of Harbour Parade, where Pizza Express is today.

Inevitably, the evening was ridiculed. The satirist George Cruikshank produced a hugely unflattering cartoon entitled *Nosing the Nob at Ramsgate* – Lady Curtis entertaining King George IV late into the night on his overnight stay at Cliff House in 1821.

A Cruikshank caricature of Sir William Curtis, Ramsgate's most important resident. (National Portrait Gallery)

Above left: The site of Cliff House, Sir William Curtis's Ramsgate residence.

Above right: Maria Fitzherbert, who George IV went back to after rejecting Caroline.

Next morning the king and Curtis paraded in open carriages to the harbour, where Curtis, in his sumptuously appointed yacht *Emma*, joined the king's fleet as they sailed for Calais. In future years he would accompany George IV on other royal visits, notably to Scotland. While he might be ridiculed in the country at large, Sir William had the respect of Ramsgate. When he died in 1829, every shop closed in his honour, and thousands followed his funeral cortege. There is a memorial to him in St George's Church, Church Hill.

Caroline's Previous Dalliance in Ramsgate

Caroline had not always favoured Dover over Ramsgate. In 1803, estranged from George, then Prince of Wales, she used East Cliff Lodge as a summer residence. The house would later be home to Lord Keith, as explored in chapter 3. Caroline was rumoured to have had numerous affairs, with the strongest evidence being against a naval officer, Captain Thomas Manby. If proven, this would have been high treason on Manby's part.

In 1806 George III, at the request of the Prince of Wales, ordered an inquiry into rumours that one of Caroline's affairs had resulted in the birth of a child, and Capt Manby was the key suspect.

A servant, Fanny Lloyd, said in a statement:

> I was at Ramsgate with the Princess in 1803. One morning when we were in the house at East Cliff, somebody, I don't recollect who, knocked at my door, and desired me to prepare breakfast for the Princess ... I slept in the housekeeper's room, on the ground floor. I opened the shutters of the window for light. I knew at that time that Captain Manby's ship was in the Downs [off Ramsgate]. When I opened the shutters, I saw the Princess, walking down the gravel walk towards the sea ... The gentleman the Princess was with was a tall man. I was surprised to see the Princess walking with a gentleman at that time in the morning. I am sure it was the Princess.

Manby swore on oath that he had never, at 'Ramsgate, East Cliff, or anywhere else, ever [slept] in any house occupied by, or belonging to, HRH the Princess of Wales.'

The commissioners decided the main accusation against the princess was unfounded. They concluded that the servant's evidence was hearsay, that the gifts and letters she sent to Manby were evidence simply of her gratitude at Manby taking two boys from a charity she patronised on his ship, the *Africaine*, and his many visits to her were merely to report on their progress.

A Refuge in Ramsgate for the Abandoned Duchess of Sussex

Relationship problems of a different kind dogged another royal Ramsgate resident, Lady Augusta Murray, who in 1817 bought Mount Albion House in Arklow Square, which now bears the address No. 22 Victoria Road.

Lady Augusta Murray, abandoned wife of the Duke of Sussex, sixth son of George III.

Lady Augusta Murray's home, Mount Albion House in Arklow Square, now No. 22 Victoria Road.

While she lived here, Augusta styled herself the Duchess of Sussex, but the title masked a very unpleasant experience of being married into the Hanovarian royal family.

In 1792, in Rome, Augusta had met and secretly married Frederick Augustus, sixth son of George III and brother to the future George IV and William IV. A second marriage ceremony was conducted in London the following year, but the couple did not reveal their full identities. Because these ceremonies had been conducted without the consent of the Crown, they contravened the Royal Marriages Act of 1772, enacted at George III's instigation to stop his sons entering into what he considered unsuitable alliances.

They had two children, Frederick and Emma, but in 1801 the marriage was annulled. George III disapproved of the liaison, and Frederick was bribed with the promise of the title Earl of Sussex, and a higher allowance, to foresake his wife. Augusta had no right to use the title Duchess of Sussex, but she did so anyway. As she needed some form of married name, Lady Augusta was given royal licence to use the surname D'Ameland, and her children D'Este, both names relating to the family's ancestry.

Various places in Ramsgate mark Augusta and her family's connection with the town. They include Augusta Road on the East Cliff, and Augusta Steps, which run from the end of that road down to the beach. D'Este Road, just to the east of Augusta Road, refers to the children's new family name, and Truro Road, which runs east from Augusta Road and links with D'Este Road, remembers Augusta's daughter Emma, who married Baron Truro.

Above: The D'Este family mausoleum, St Laurence's churchyard, where Lady Augusta is buried.

left: Augusta Steps on the East Cliff, named after Lady Augusta Murray. (Nick Barham)

Lady D'Ameland, as Augusta then was, lived in Ramsgate until her death in 1830. Her son Frederick had a mausoleum built for his mother in the graveyard of St Laurence's Church. In addition to Lady Augusta, the D'Este Mausoleum holds the remains of her parents, the Earl and Countess of Dunmore, Emma, her husband Baron Truro and Frederick himself.

DID YOU KNOW?
The ship from which pirate Radio Caroline broadcast, the MV *Ross Revenge*, drifted onto the Goodwin Sands in 1991, ending the era of offshore pirate radio in the English Channel.

How Princess Victoria Almost Died in Ramsgate

Victoria first came to Ramsgate in 1823, aged four. She returned regularly through her childhood with her mother, the widowed Duchess of Kent, and grew to love the town. She stayed variously at Townley House, Chatham Street; at Albion House, now the Albion House Hotel in Albion Square; and at West Cliff House, off Pegwell Road, where her pet donkey is said to have died, and was buried in the garden.

East Cliff Lodge comes back into the story of royal Ramsgate once again with Victoria. Sir Moses Montefiore, who bought the house in 1831, gave the princess a golden key, allowing her to enjoy his 24-acre grounds whenever she wished.

Princess Victoria. (The Wellcome Collection)

Above left: Albion House, now a hotel, where Victoria almost died. (Nick Barham)

Above right: The plaque recording Victoria's stay at Albion House.

Life for the princess was less regimented in Ramsgate, and she was occasionally allowed to play on the sands with her dog and mix with other children. Discipline, however, was still maintained, despite Victoria's status as a princess. When, at Townley House, she spilt a full inkwell on the floor at the top of the grand main staircase, she was made to scrub it clean. When the house was a girls' school in the early twentieth century, a brass plaque recorded the incident as a deterrent to clumsiness.

DID YOU KNOW?
Arthur Ransome, author of the *Swallows and Amazons* series, was inspired by a child he saw wearing a red cap in Ramsgate's Royal Harbour to give similar headgear to his Amazon pirate girls Nancy and Peggy Blackett.

Victoria's affection for Ramsgate is shown by the fact that she later bought *Ramsgate Sands*, by W. P. Frith, a painting that gives a lively impression of life at the Victorian-era seaside resort, and which is now in the Royal Collection at Buckingham Palace.

However, Victoria's life in the town was not always idyllic. In 1835, aged sixteen, and two years before she would become queen, the princess fell dangerously ill with typhoid fever while staying at Albion House, and came close to death.

As Lucy Worsley writes in *Queen Victoria: Daughter, Wife, Mother, Widow,* Victoria's mother and her senior advisor, Sir John Conroy, put her condition down to teenage sulks and temper tantrums, despite Victoria being too sick to leave her room for a fortnight. Her doctor, James Clark, was called to Ramsgate but was persuaded her condition was not serious and left.

Rumours of Victoria's grave condition abounded, but when the local press noticed she had not been seen in public for several days, they were told the princess had just 'a slight cold'. In a statement, Conroy later insisted: 'All the stories you will have read of the Princess's illness were not true. She was never confined to her bed or to her bedroom. She was never carried up or down stairs, or shaded with screens, never having had any beatings in her limbs.'

He was lying. On 9 October Victoria's fever rose dangerously and delirium set in. As Worsley relates, typhoid fever was a terrible illness: 'A victim turns deathly pale, vomits blood, and has vicious diarrhoea.' She had probably contracted it through drinking infected water or milk.

Finally, the Duchess of Kent and Victoria's tutor, Louise Lehzen, could no longer stand to see her suffering. Dr David Plenderleath, a single man of forty-four, was summoned from his home in Nelson Crescent. Worsley says he was rushed up the stairs and 'was very grave' on seeing how sick Victoria was. After his visit, the princess's condition stabilised. Perhaps 'simply as a result of having been taken seriously', the crisis was over. She was treated with quinine to bring down her fever, and her strong constitution fought the salmonella bacteria that had poisoned her digestive system.

By 31 October Victoria was well enough to write in her journal again, but in the five weeks she had been confined to her room her hair had fallen out and she had lost muscle and mobility. It was not until January 1836 that she fully recovered. Fortunately, Victoria's illness did not sour her opinion of Ramsgate, and she returned many times as queen.

Queen Victoria. (The Welcome Collection)

5. Ramsgate the Resort, and Its Famous Visitors

Ramsgate in Its Heyday

The poet Samuel Taylor Coleridge coined a word for enjoying the delights of this distinguished seaside resort: 'Ramsgatise'. On 31 October 1821 he wrote to a friend from the town: 'O I wish, you were here, and that we could all Ramsgatise till the midst of December.'

To Ramsgatise meant to take a grand house – ideally on Wellington Crescent, Nelson Crescent or Royal Crescent – from August to October. To fill that house with family and friends, plus servants of course, and to revel in the camaraderie and conversation. To swim before breakfast, and then to socialise in the bath houses, libraries or assembly rooms. To stroll along the clifftop promenades or around the harbour and to know, from observing how absolutely anyone who was anyone was also here, that you were in the most fashionable place you could possibly be. Coleridge preferred Ramsgate in the autumn, but summer was the peak season.

Bustling Harbour Parade in the early years of the twentieth century.

An aerial view showing elegant Albion Place, later severely bomb damaged.

The newly constructed Royal Parade, which greatly enhanced Ramsgate's imposing seafront.

Above left: Samuel Taylor Coleridge. (The Wellcome Collection)

Above right: A blue plaque marking one of Coleridge's holiday homes, at No. 3 Wellington Crescent.

Wellington Crescent. Coleridge stayed variously at Nos 3, 7, 28 and 29.

Ramsgate in its nineteenth-century heyday attracted royalty, as we have seen, plus illustrious visitors ranging from the Prime Minister, Lord Liverpool, and the foreign secretary, George Canning, to the most distinguished literary figures including Wilkie Collins and Jane Austen. Charles Dickens, who preferred Broadstairs, was nevertheless drawn to rumbustious Ramsgate for the sheer spectacle to be observed and absorbed.

Towering figures from Charles Darwin to Karl Marx and Frederick Engels came to take the waters. Many are remembered in the blue plaques dotted around the town, but here we shall concentrate on the lesser-known stories connected with them.

Coleridge, author of 'The Rime of the Ancient Mariner' and one of our greatest poets, came numerous times between 1819, when he was forty-seven, and 1833 – the year before he died – staying variously at Nos 3, 7, 28 and 29 Wellington Crescent, Nos 1, 8 and 9 Plains of Waterloo and elsewhere. The fifty letters he wrote from here give an illuminating account of the resort at its peak.

DID YOU KNOW?
The very naturalistic rock formations on Madeira Walk, the Western Undercliff Chine and Winterstoke Gardens are actually a man-made substance, pulhamite. It was invented by James Pulham in the nineteenth century and is a blend of sand, cement and ash applied over a core of crushed brick and rubble. Pulhamite, used in 1894 to create Madeira Walk's mini Swiss chine and waterfall and at the other locations in the 1920s and '30s, was so realistic that it even fooled some geologists.

Ramsgate began to really take off once the Napoleonic Wars ended in 1815, with the biggest breakthrough coming in 1826, when a regular steam packet service operated from London. Why spend a day in a cramped, rattling carriage to get to Brighton when you could cruise in comfort to Ramsgate in a few hours? By 1837, when Victoria came to the throne, the clifftops were lined with elegant terraces, crescents and squares, all built for visitors.

Charles Dickens vividly captured the scene as a steam packet delivered its cargo at Ramsgate, in one of his sketches by Boz, published in 1837:

> The sun was shining brightly; the sea, dancing to its own music, rolled merrily in; crowds of people promenaded to and fro; young ladies tittered, old ladies talked; nursemaids displayed their charms to the greatest possible advantages; and their little charges ran up and down and to and fro under the feet and between the legs of the assembled concourse ... There were old gentlemen trying to make out objects through long telescopes, and young ones making objects of themselves in open shirt collars; ladies carrying about portable chairs, and portable chairs carrying about invalids; parties waiting on the pier for parties who had come by the steam boat and nothing was to be heard but talking, laughing, welcoming, and merriment.

A remarkably realistic artificial rock called pulhamite was used at Madeira Walk. (Nick Barham)

Charles Dickens wrote vividly of steam-packet travellers arriving at Ramsgate. (The Wellcome Collection)

The steam packet *Royal Sovereign* entering Ramsgate Royal Harbour.

Sea Bathing

Health was the first draw, with swimming and drinking seawater recommended for almost any ailment. Coleridge had many. As a child, he had contracted rheumatic fever and, as an adult, suffered from depression and repeated bouts of crippling anxiety. He was treated with laudanum, which led to a lifelong addiction to opium. He had also endured a broken marriage, and a long but unrequited love affair.

He was an early advocate of what might today be called wild swimming. In 1819 he wrote to a friend describing having 'a glorious tumble in the waves' at Dumpton Gap, between Ramsgate and Broadstairs, though he would have preferred the water to be colder:

> My bath is ... but a very pleasant walk along the top of the cliff from which you descend through a steep lane cut thro' the chalk rocks – the tide comes up to the end of the lane, and washes the cliff; but a little before or a little after high tide there are nice clean seats of rock with footbaths, and then an expanse of sand greater than I need, and exactly a hundred of my strides from the end of the lane there is a good roomy arched cavern, with an oven or cupboard in it where one's clothes may be put free from the sand...

Most visitors would have been appalled at such an experience, and much preferred to conduct their sea bathing from the bathing machines lined up on the sands to the east

Bathing machines lined up on Ramsgate Sands.

of Ramsgate Harbour. In her *Memoirs of a Highland Lady,* Elizabeth Grant described the scene there in 1811:

> Early in the morning we all went down to the sands to bathe in a respectable manner, suited to a crowded watering place. A little table on which lay a great book stood within a railing enclosing all of the bathing machines. Each party, on entering the gates of this enclosure, set their names down in the book, and in their turn were conducted to a bathing machine, roomy boxes on wheels, shaded at one end by a large canvas hood that reached the water when the horse at the other end had proceeded with it to sufficient depth.
>
> The driver then turned his carriage round with the hood to the sea, and unhinging his traces went in search of another fare, leaving the bathers to the care of a woman in the blue flannel jacket and petticoat and a straw bonnet, who soon waded into view from another machine, lifted up the canvas shade and stood ready to assist in the fearful plunge.
>
> The shock of death was always an agony. That over, we would have ducked about much longer than the woman let us. It was rather frightful bathing when the waves were high, at least to the timid ones. Some people went into the sea when they really might have been carried away by it, when they and the women had to keep hold of the ropes as the waves went over them.

When the Sea Cure Failed...

The sea cure didn't always work. Karl Marx and Friedrich Engels, authors of the *Communist Manifesto,* regularly visited Ramsgate for their health, Marx staying often in Abott's Hill, a modest street behind Albion Place, and also at No. 6 Artillery Road.

Bob Simmonds in *Weather Here, Wish You Were Lovely: A History of Holidaying in Ramsgate* writes that Marx came for three weeks in 1874, suffering from a combination of insomnia and carbuncles. Simmonds notes: 'Despite the "marvellous air" and adhering to a regime of bathing, walking and careful diet he wrote to his daughter that "my condition is even worse than in London" and "I have not yet managed to get a good night's sleep".'

In July and August 1877, Engels stayed at No. 2 Adelaide Gardens with his long-term mistress Lydia Burns, who was suffering from an undiagnosed ailment that later proved to be cancer. Poignantly he wrote to Marx: 'The magic powers of sea bathing have failed her for the first time.' Sadly, Lizzie died the following year, but not before Engels had married her. He later wrote of her: 'My wife was a real child of the Irish proletariat and her passionate devotion to the class in which she was born was worth much more to me – and helped me more in times of stress – than all the elegance of an educated, artistic middle-class bluestocking.'

In 1850, Charles and Emma Darwin brought their daughter Annie to Ramsgate for sea-bathing treatments, staying at No. 8 Paragon. As Edna Healey relates in *Emma Darwin: The Wife of an Inspirational Genius,* the Darwins' bright and lively daughter had become weak and listless. While Charles collected sea shells, Emma watched the bathing woman take Annie out to the waves in a bathing machine, but in the chill October air she caught flu and the family went home to Downe, near Orpington. Seawater treatments continued there, but the following year Annie died of scarlet fever.

Above left: Charles Darwin brought his daughter Annie to Ramsgate for the sea cure. (The Wellcome Collection)

Above right: Darwin's holiday home at No. 8 Paragon.

Hotels, Bath Houses, Libraries and Assembly Rooms

The season was highly organised, with masters of ceremonies employed to ensure decorum. These were often military men, including Colonel Isaac Clarke, who had led the charge of the Royal Scots Greys at the Battle of Waterloo.

As Alan Clayson notes in *Wish You Were Here,* these were powerful men. 'It was one of the roles of the masters of ceremonies to enforce bathing etiquette, the major concern being to ensure that the sexes bathed in different areas or at different times.' They met the steam packets, noted who was arriving and selected those thought suitable for the assembly rooms and libraries, where much of the entertainment took place. 'In the assemblies they upheld the decorum of the ball-room and the strict rules obtaining in the card rooms; their authority was absolute.'

DID YOU KNOW?
In 1955 Peter Darby, a Chatham House schoolboy, started a jazz club in the cellars of Granville House, as the Granville Hotel was by then known, and formed The Cavemen's Jazz Band to play there each Saturday night, with a strictly soft drinks-only bar and cardboard egg trays on the walls to prevent complaints about noise. Entry was restricted to under-twenty-ones, and Peter's headmaster popped in regularly to keep an eye on things.

In Margate the assembly rooms had a fixed location in the Royal Hotel, Cecil Square. In Ramsgate they fluctuated between the smartest hotels: The Royal Hotel and The Royal Albion Hotel and adjacent East Indian and American Coffee House.

The Royal Hotel and Albion Hotel, locations for the all-important assembly rooms.

The Royal pub now replaces the Royal Hotel, and Pizza Express occupies the building that replaced the Albion Hotel.

The Royal Hotel, formerly the Kings Head Tavern, was at No. 46 Harbour Parade, where The Royal pub now stands. The Royal Albion stood close by, on the other side of Albion Hill, but was demolished in 1894 when Madeira Walk was built, creating a wide thoroughfare up to East Cliff.

While the richest visitors did not stay at the hotels, they were the places where grand balls and functions were held.

Refined visitors preferred to bathe indoors in the comfort of bath houses. Among the most popular were those of Isaac Dyason, on the quayside at the edge of the inner marina.

The *New Margate, Ramsgate and Broadstairs Guide* described it as having: 'four baths for warm sea-water, also a plunging and shower bath, which are so well contrived as to have a continual supply from every tide; attached to them are very convenient waiting and dressing rooms; the whole are completed on such a plan as to be much approved and recommended.'

In 1855 Dyason moved to new premises built on the area of the old Royal Albion Hotel not used for Madeira Walk, creating the Royal Clarence Baths, now Pizza Express.

In 1816 the Isabella Baths opened on the West Cliff at the end of the Paragon. *The New Margate, Ramsgate and Broadstairs Guide* described just how impressive it was:

> All the baths are formed of white marble, and the dimensions of the celebrated warm baths of Naples ... they are placed in a room lighted and ventilated from the ceiling; the dressing rooms which communicate with them are of an ample size and fitted up with everything that can administer to the comfort and pleasure of the bathers ...
>
> A horizontal funnel, in which the tide ebbs and flows, has been excavated in the chalk rock, and runs under the building until it joins with the vertical funnel containing the pumps and pipes which raise the water to the reservoir on the top, from which it is

conveyed by pipes to the boilers and other parts of the buildings. The pumps are worked by horses, and are so placed as always to get their supply at high water.

Bob Simmonds says, in *Weather is here, wish you were lovely!*, that the Isabella Baths were later known as the Royal Kent Baths, under the patronage of the Duchess of Kent, but were replaced in 1862 by the Paragon Hotel, now the Churchill Tavern. A new Royal Paragon Baths was built at the foot of the cliffs beside the harbour.

There were also baths between the sands and Kent Terrace. These developed from a simple area of sheds used as waiting rooms for bathers but were developed by Barling, Float and Wells, becoming known as the Royal Victoria Baths in 1847.

Another key element of Ramsgate's attractions was its public libraries. These offered far more than the loan of books. They were places of general entertainment, hosting concerts and recitals. There was modest gambling, and coffee rooms in which to relax, socialise and catch up with the news. They had extensive shops selling stationery, jewellery, perfumes and souvenirs.

'The principal library', wrote William Kidd in his *Picturesque Pocket Companion*, 'belongs to Messrs. Burgess and Hunt', and was in Market Place, on the corner of High Street and Queen Street, where Lloyds Bank now stands.

Coleridge, who could not afford the subscription to the assembly rooms, haunted this library. He cut a strange and instantly recognisable figure. Allan Clayson relates one account of an observer who 'had heard an elderly gentleman in the public library who looked like a dissenting minister, talking as she had never heard man talk. Like his own Ancient Mariner, when he had at once fixed your eye he held you spellbound.'

The Churchill Tavern, on the site of the Royal Kent Baths. (Nick Barham)

Kent Terrace, site of the Royal Victoria Baths.

Another establishment, Sackett and Fuller's Marine Library, was on the West Cliff at Sion Hill. Kidd says of it: 'The evening musical promenade is held here, [featuring] ... excellent music, executed by good performers, in a pleasing and masterly manner. Over the library is a very superior boarding-house, which is pleasantly situate, commanding an extensive sea view, and overlooking the beautiful gardens of Sir William Curtis,' at Cliff House.

The 1864 guidebook *All About Ramsgate and Broadstairs* reported:

> It unites in itself all the advantages of a library, a bazaar, a music hall and an innocent gambling house ... You may skim over a novel then hear a sweet ballad, and afterwards wildly stake a shilling in the raffle; and, should you win become the happy possessor of a cake of soap, a bottle of hair oil, a wooden spade, or any other *objet de luxe* of low price.
>
> There is no difficulty in finding out the Marine Library of an evening, for its advertising piano may be heard for fifty yard off. On the occasion of our first visit we had only to follow the polka; and soon found ourselves standing in front of a large square building, with closed French shutters before the tall windows in the ground-floor, and the light streaking out, through the cracks, as though the place were on fire. The crowd entered and came out again as if an auction were going on...
>
> 'Mr Fuller ... the polite and neatly-attired proprietor – stood at a table covered with green baize, and looked around, searching for gamblers. The worthy gentleman was surrounded by a mob of ladies, some making up their minds to "have a try", others tired of losing, yet unable to tear themselves away from the fascinating board.

A Place for Scandal

Jane Austen knew Ramsgate well, but was aware of its dangers. The practice of women bathing in the nude could attract the wrong sort of man to the resort, despite the fact the hoods of the bathing machines were supposed to protect ladies' modesty.

Austen holidayed here with her extended family in 1803 and 1804, renting Nos 7 and 8 Sion Hill. In 1806 her brother Frank, later Admiral Sir Francis Austen, married a local girl, Mary Gibson. Frank was stationed here during the Napoleonic Wars as commander of the North Foreland unit of the Sea Fencibles, a sort of home guard that would have sprung into action should Napoleon have managed to land at Pegwell Bay.

Austen chose to set scenes in Ramsgate in her 1831 novel *Pride and Prejudice,* in which Mr Wickham, a compulsive gambler, libertine and rake, attempts to seduce fifteen-year-old Georgiana Darcy, younger sister of Mr Fitzwilliam Darcy, and get his hands on her £30,000 fortune.

Georgiana, a shy and withdrawn adolescent, is supposed to be chaperoned by a Mrs Young, her tutor, but Young has had a previous relationship with Wickham and 'by her connivance and aid, he so far recommended himself to Georgiana, whose affectionate heart retained a strong impression of his kindness to her as a child, that she was persuaded to believe herself in love, and to consent to an elopement.' Mr Darcy acted in the nick of time and saved her.

Wilkie Collins, who wrote *The Woman in White* during a year-long stay at No. 9 or 10 Wellington Crescent in 1859, brought his complicated private life to Ramsgate.

Collins had long-standing relationships with two women: Caroline Graves, and Martha Rudd, with whom he had three children. Collins, who had been a regular visitor to the town since boyhood, often had his two partners staying separately in Ramsgate – Caroline Graves regularly lodged at No. 14 Nelson Crescent, Martha and the children at No. 27 Wellington Crescent. Collins would move between the two houses, calling himself William Dawson when with Martha.

In *The Secret Life of Wilkie Collins,* William M. Clarke quotes him explaining to a friend that when he arrived in Ramsgate from London with Martha: 'Wilkie Collins of 82 Wimpole Street had disappeared from this mortal sphere of action and is replaced by William Dawson, 27 Wellington Crescent, Ramsgate. In plain English I am here with my "morganatic family" – and must travel (like the Royal Personages) under an alias – or not be admitted into their respectable house now occupied by my children and their mother.'

Samuel Taylor Coleridge also attracted rumours in Ramsgate because of his unconventional holiday arrangements. Since 1816 he had been living in Highgate, north London, with a young doctor and his wife, James and Ann Gillman. The arrangement gave Coleridge the stability his earlier life had lacked, and he greatly benefited from it.

Each year he would holiday in Ramsgate with the Gillmans or, rather, with Ann Gillman. Her husband would stay for just a few days before returning to London.

In 1824 the gossipy essayist Charles Lamb spread a rumour in literary circles that Coleridge was living in open adultery with Ann, while insisting he thought the idea preposterous. As Allan Clayson comments in *Wish You Were Here,* 'which is not, however, a guarantee that the rumour was wholly without foundation. Coleridge was well aware

Right: One of Wilkie Collins' partners, Martha Rudd, stayed with their children at No. 27 Wellington Crescent.

Below: Wilkie Collins' other partner, Caroline Graves, stayed at No. 14 Nelson Crescent.

that his presence in Ramsgate with Mrs Gillman while her husband was back at Highgate would give rise to such talk. For appearance sake, if nothing else, no holiday went by without the careful chaperoning of Mrs Gillman.'

Friends had long noted Coleridge's open admiration for Ann, a pretty, blue-eyed blonde seven years his junior. In the long periods she and Coleridge were in Ramsgate without James, husband and wife rarely wrote to each other. Rather, Coleridge wrote constantly to each, passing on messages between husband and wife.

Whatever the truth of the arrangement, it appears to have suited all parties.

Ramsgate in Decline

Ironically, given that Ramsgate's cachet had come to depend so much on Queen Victoria's endorsement, the resort began a long, slow decline soon after she came to the throne in 1937. The railway, which arrived in 1846, made the town accessible to a far wider social mix, and it lost its exclusivity. Then, in 1848, Dover opened its superior harbour, taking much of its marine trade.

The railway came right down to the beach, in a tunnel cut from Dumpton Gap that emerged on the sands to the east of the harbour, dispensing visitors straight on to the beach.

Trains brought Ramsgate visitors right down onto the beach.

Above and right: Karl Marx stayed at No. 56 Plains of Waterloo in 1879.

In 1876 Frederic Engels wrote to Karl Marx bemoaning the arrival of the *petit bourgeoise*:

> At this moment Ramsgate is populated almost exclusively by small greengrocers and quite small shopkeepers from London. These people stay here for a week, for as long as the return ticket is valid, and then make room for others of the same ilk. It's the former day-trip public which now takes a week off. At first sight one would think they were working men, but their conversation immediately betrays the fact they are "rather above that" and belong to quite the most disagreeable stratum of London society.

Undeterred, Marx came back in 1879, staying at the more salubrious No. 56 Plains of Waterloo.

Tellingly, Charles Dickens chose to set his story around a newly rich Cockney family struggling to acquire gentility, *The Tuggses at Ramsgate,* in the town. The hapless Tuggses, who chose Ramsgate over Gravesend – 'low' – and Margate – 'nobody here, but tradespeople' – get swindled out of their newly acquired riches by a posh conman.

Mr Tuggs is one of Engels' despised greengrocers. Yet Dickens was no snob, and seems to have presented this as a cautionary tale, for he enjoyed Ramsgate and the vibrant popular culture he found here. He attended George Sanger's Amphitheatre, which stood on the corner of High Street and George Street, where circus and music hall acts played. Paul Schlicke, in *Dickens and Popular Entertainment,* writes that in 1846 Dickens 'was caught in a "whirl of dissipation" upon discovering a female lion tamer', Ellen Chapman, soon to become Sanger's wife. 'He wrote to [a friend] "That you should have been and gone and missed last Saturday! Wild beasts, too, in Ramsgate, and a young lady in armour, as goes into dens, while a rustic keeper who speaks through his nose exclaims, *Behold the abazid power of woobbud!*"'

George Cruikshank's illustration for Charles Dickens' tale *The Tuggses at Ramsgate.*

'Seriously', Dickens went on, 'she beats van Amburgh [an American animal trainer who had developed the first trained wild animal act]. And I think the Duke of Wellington must have her painted by Landseer.'

The New Resort of St Lawrence-on-Sea

Not everyone accepted that Ramsgate was past its best. In 1863 a group of local businessmen led by Edward Pugin, son of the more renowned Augustus Welby Pugin, who we shall meet in chapter 6, set out to build a whole new resort on the clifftop to the east of Wellington Crescent, which would attract rich visitors all year round.

St Lawrence-on-Sea would counter Ramsgate's decline, and re-establish its exclusivity. Its jewel in the crown was to be a grand new terrace of houses. When the houses did not sell, they became the Granville Hotel.

Charles G. Harper in *The Kentish Coast* wrote at the time: 'The Granville does things on a lordly scale, and has an express of its own from London. Down below it, indeed, and in direct communication, is the railway station, on the sands beneath the cliffs.'

Visitors coming on the non-stop Granville Express from London Victoria would find a spa offering twenty-five different types of bath. It was claimed the *table d'hote* in its great Gothic dining hall was 'universally acknowledged as the best dinner in the Kingdom'. There was a theatre and a grand ballroom.

Architect Edward Pugin's bust outside the former Granville Hotel.

Promenaders were charged to walk past the Granville Hotel.

The former toll booth, where strollers paid to walk along the promenade.

Granville Terrace was built to the east of the hotel, with five of the houses later becoming the Hotel St Cloud.

Pugin went bankrupt in 1873, but the Granville was saved by Edmund Davies, who had developed the exclusive Thanet resort of Westgate-on-Sea. He built a promenade and clifftop gardens – complete with a toll booth to charge non-residents who wanted to walk through – and the Granville Marina at the bottom of the cliffs. He cut a long sloping access road and a huge retaining wall on Marine Parade.

John Huddlestone, in *400 Facts and Curiosities of Ramsgate,* wrote: 'The Granville Marina was in turn a concert room, a skating rink, a theatre, and eventually the first place in Ramsgate at which cinematograph pictures were exhibited. The Marine Hall, or, as it was called The Garden By The Sea, had many vicissitudes until [post-First World War] days, when it was taken over by Messrs. Tomson and Wotton [Ramsgate brewers who] ... transformed it into one of the most popular places of entertainment on the south coast.' Alongside it they built a 'magnificent modern bathing pool ... one of the finest in England'.

The station closed in 1926 when, says Huddlestone, it was replaced by 'one of the largest amusement halls on the South Coast, Merrie England, which can cater for thousands of visitors in wet or fine weather. The Long Bar in this building is one of the longest bars in Great Britain, and possibly Europe.'

The bathing pool, built by Ramsgate brewers Tomson and Wotton.

6. Pugin and Montefiore: Building Jerusalem in Ramsgate

Left: St Augustine's Church alongside The Grange, Pugin's family home.

Below: Sir Moses Montefiore's house, East Cliff Lodge.

EAST CLIFF VILLA, RAMSGATE, THE RESIDENCE OF SIR MOSES MONTEFIORE.

Ramsgate Synagogue, built by Sir Moses Montefiore. (Nick Barham)

Two remarkable men with a great deal in common but a key religious difference were building empires at opposite ends of Ramsgate in the 1840s.

On the West Cliff, Augustus Welby Pugin, best known for designing the interiors to the Palace of Westminster, was creating St Augustine's Church, complete with graveyard, priest's house, cloister and schoolroom, plus a house for himself, The Grange. His church is his monument and final resting place.

On the East Cliff, Sir Moses Montefiore, stockbroker, campaigner, philanthropist and one of the richest men in England, had made his home in East Cliff Lodge, a house that had already played a distinguished part in the story of Ramsgate. Alongside it he went on to create a synagogue, a theological college and a mausoleum in which he and his wife Judith are buried.

Both men were drawn to Jerusalem, and both are buried facing east, towards the holy city. Montefiore travelled there often, and constructed a famous Kent-style windmill outside the old city, along with almshouses, designed and built by Ramsgate craftsmen. After Pugin's death, his son Edward built St Augustine's Monastery in Jerusalem.

The big difference between these two men – towering figures in Victorian England – was that Pugin was Catholic and Montefiore was Jewish. Yet in a way this difference united them. As Father Marcus Holden, then parish priest at St Augustine's, explained in a talk given at Ramsgate's Comfort Inn in 2017, they were both members of minority religions whose followers had only gained political emancipation during their lifetimes. They were outside the establishment and had to fight prejudice and discrimination, both in Ramsgate and in their wider lives.

Both had foreign roots: Pugin's father fled France at the time of the revolution, Montefiore was born in Livorno, Italy, and both chose Ramsgate to realise their great visions. Both, Marcus Holden explained, were seeking to recreate Jerusalem in Ramsgate.

Yet, despite both being involved in the Great Exhibition of 1851 and living within a few miles of each other, there is no record that they ever met.

Today, in Ramsgate, the legacies of these two great men are widely divergent.

Pugin's church now houses the Shrine of St Augustine and National Pugin Centre, and is hence the official place to honour the saint's mission to establish Christianity in Anglo-Saxon England. After a period of decline and neglect, Pugin's creation is carefully nurtured, and his reputation has never been higher. Support from the Heritage Lottery Fund has enabled the establishment of the visitor centre, a place for education and research, in the original schoolroom. It is visited by pilgrims, Pugin enthusiasts and scholars. His house, The Grange, has been restored by the Landmark Trust as a holiday home.

East Cliff it is a very different story. East Cliff Lodge, badly damaged while occupied by the army during the Second World War, was sold to Ramsgate council in 1952 and demolished in 1954. Only the outbuildings survive today. The extensive grounds are the public King George VI Memorial Park. The synagogue is behind high walls and locked gates, and services are only held here occasionally. The theological college was also demolished.

Let us look in detail at what Montefiore and Pugin achieved in Ramsgate, and what their lives here were like.

Above left: The imposing font Pugin designed for his church.

Above right: Inside Sir Moses Montefiore's Ramsgate Synagogue. (Courtesy of Srsai under Creative Commons 3.0)

Augustus Welby Pugin's tomb in St Augustine's Church.

Sir Moses Montefiore's mausoleum, where he and his wife Judith are buried. (Nick Barham)

Augustus Welby Pugin, a Prophet Without Honour in Ramsgate

Pugin, born in 1812, first came to Ramsgate aged sixteen, staying with his maternal aunt, Selina Welby, at Rose Hill Cottage, Rose Hill. In 1832 he stayed with her again, seeking solace after the death of his first wife, Anne Garnett. At twenty, Pugin was a widower with a small baby.

After the death of his parents within four months of each other, he returned to Ramsgate with his new wife Louise to be near his aunt, renting Ellington Cottage at No. 188 Grange Road in St Lawrence. To his dismay, Pugin found in Ramsgate 'a most barren spot for Catholic ideas'. The remains of the medieval past were neglected. Minister Abbey in particular, he said, was 'going to absolute ruin'.

Pugin moved away for a few years but, says Rosemary Hill, in *Pugin and Ramsgate*: 'The associations of Ramsgate with his own family, with St Augustine, his patron saint, and the powerful attraction of the sea, which he loved to watch as well as to sail, all combined to draw him back.'

He returned to build a church and house from which he could look down on Pegwell Bay and St Augustine's landing point at Ebbsfleet.

Hill says that Pugin chose to realise here the 'dream of rebuilding medieval Catholic England'. A vision of 'work and home, art and love as part of the same complete Christian ideal'. And he wrote a book, *The True Principles of Pointed or Christian Architecture,* which made it plain that the Gothic style he championed, and which became the defining architecture of the Victorian period, was not mere style or fashion. It was the concrete manifestation of a resurgent faith: Catholicism.

Rose Hill Cottage, the first place Augustus Welby Pugin stayed in Ramsgate.

Pugin created stunning interiors at his home, The Grange. (The Landmark Trust)

Rosemary Hill, in *God's Architect*, says that what Pugin built in Ramsgate was 'a model not just for architecture but for society, for a coherent, Christian civic order in which the poor would be fed, the old cared for, the children taught.' His house, The Grange, became the model for the many thousands of substantial family villas that spread across Victorian suburbia.

DID YOU KNOW?

Augustus Welby Pugin had a half share in a lugger, *Caroline*, which he used to rescue shipwrecked sailors and salvage cargoes. He would watch from the tower of The Grange as ships foundered on the Goodwin Sands. During one storm he wrote: 'it is thick at sea, so perhaps something will run on the sands ... a homeward bound Batavia man [a ship of the Dutch East India Company] would be just the thing.' In letters he mentioned the salvage value of gin, ebony, tea and coconuts and said of the *Caroline*: 'as a source of income she seems to have more than earned her keep.'

Not everyone in Ramsgate approved of what Pugin was doing. In many ways he was a prophet without honour in his home town. He was a controversial and sometimes hated figure here, and there were outbreaks of violence directed against him.

In 1845 a naval man, Lieutenant Hutchinson, of The Shrubbery, Vale Square, went into battle against Pugin. He raised £8,000 and commissioned George Gilbert Scott to build Christ Church in Vale Square, yet he built it in imitation of Pugin's style.

Rosemary Hill says: 'Thus it was, ironically, that the church in Ramsgate which most reflects Pugin's influence was built in a direct attempt to counter it. Almost within sight of one another Christ Church and St Augustine's rose simultaneously.'

Christ Church's first vicar, Edward Hoare, described Pugin as the 'devil incarnate', and a war of competitive philanthropy was fought between the two.

While Pugin struggled to establish his modest school, and closed it when he found the 'little beasts' had been stealing his coal, Christ Church raised enough to build one for 450 pupils in Royal Road.

There was rivalry, too, over the welfare of sailors. Both Pugin and Hutchinson and Hoare wanted to establish a hospital for them. While the Christ Church faction successfully raised the funds for the non-denominational Ramsgate Seamen's Infirmary, Pugin's Catholic-only home in King Street failed.

In November 1850, Ramsgate was swept up in a national crisis known as the Papal Aggression, a reaction to the restoration of a Catholic Church hierarchy in England. Anglicans across the country felt under attack.

In Ramsgate, there were anti-Catholic posters everywhere, Brewer's drays trundled around with 'No Popery' scrawled on the beer casks they carried, and mobs gathered in the streets. While Pugin was away in London, a gang carrying an effigy of the pope attempted to march on The Grange. They were turned back by police but Pugin's wife was 'much frightened'. Some accounts have his house being pelted with excrement, the gateposts graffitied and Pugin's children and servants abused in the street.

Christ Church, whose vicar, Edward Hoare, described Pugin as the 'devil incarnate'.

Vale Square, home to Pugin's Anglican opponent, Lieutenant Hutchinson.

An incident in Pugin's private life did not help his relations with the town. In 1847, after the death of his second wife, Louisa, of rheumatic fever, Pugin fell in love with Helen Lumsdaine, the niece of his neighbour, Henry Benson of West Cliff Lodge. The Bensons were Anglican and friends of Christ Church's vicar, Edward Hoare.

During a long winter stay at her uncle's, Helen came to spend most of each day with Pugin at The Grange. After she returned home to Upper Hardres near Canterbury, where her father was vicar, they corresponded. Rosemary Hill writes in *God's Architect* that Helen's letters 'bespeak her excitement at toying with forbidden fruit'. Hill adds:

> For a country rector's daughter to correspond with a man so famous, so controversial, so clearly half in love with her, was indeed an adventure...
>
> She longed both for Pugin and to be a Catholic. She told Pugin of her decision to convert, and then her family, who were horrified. They banned her from communicating with Pugin.

Secretly they became engaged. 'Pugin urged her to come to Ramsgate and be received into the Church and then married at once privately.'

Later, Helen changed her mind but despite begging to be released from her promise, Pugin refused. He then took the extraordinary step of publishing a pamphlet detailing their affair and including her letters, which he distributed around Ramsgate.

West Cliff Lodge, where Pugin met Helen Lumsdaine, a woman he later publicly shamed.

Hill says: 'Such public exposure of a woman was, by any standards, brutal and in Victorian England amounted to an act of social violence. Pugin admitted that he hoped she would be forced to leave the country.'

In 1848 Pugin married his third wife, Jane, but by now his obsessive work rate had destroyed his health. In February 1852 he had a complete breakdown and was committed to an asylum. He recovered sufficiently to return to The Grange, but died there on 14 September, aged just forty.

Sir Moses Montefiore and Ramsgate: Centre of the Jewish World

When Moses Montefiore (1784–1885) passed through Ramsgate on his honeymoon, he and his wife Judith fell in love with the town. In 1822 they returned, first renting East Cliff Lodge and finally buying it in 1831.

By the time of his first visit here, Montefiore had made a great deal of money on the stock exchange. Working with his brother-in-law Nathan Rothschild, he helped found the Alliance Assurance Company in reaction to insurance companies which discriminated against Jews.

In Ramsgate, he and Judith were able to concentrate on the philanthropic causes that greatly interested them. In 1835, after a long engagement with the campaign for Jewish emancipation, Moses became President of the Board of Deputies of British Jews.

Abigail Green, author of *Moses Montefiore: Jewish Liberator, Imperial Hero*, says that being home to one of the most prominent Jews of the time made Ramsgate the centre of the Jewish world, and a focus for the international Jewish community.

Sir Moses Montefiore. (Alamy)

In 1833 he built the first element in his plan to nurture a vibrant Jewish community on the East Cliff: a synagogue, between Honeysuckle Road and Dumpton Park Drive, and close to East Cliff Lodge. Sharman Kadish, in her *Jewish Heritage in England*, says: 'in the manner of an English aristocrat, the Sephardi grandee built his own private 'chapel' in reticent neoclassical style';

It is a simple building with white stucco walls, a lead roof and a chiming clock, which is the only example on an English synagogue. It is inscribed in English with the motto 'Time flies virtue alone remains', but has no Hebrew or Jewish symbolism to identify the building's function.

Judith Montefiore died in 1862, leaving Moses to a long widowhood. He built a mausoleum, in which she was buried, alongside the synagogue. It is a replica of Rachel's tomb, which is on the road between Jerusalem and Bethlehem, and is a place of pilgrimage for both Jews and Muslims. It is reputed to be the place where the Matriarch Rachel was buried by her husband Jacob after she died during childbirth. The Montefiores had restored Rachel's tomb in 1839. Sir Moses saw his replica as an appropriate memorial to his childless wife. Behind the mausoleum is a pillar, which he brought back from the Holy Land, and which is believed to allude to the stone Jacob erected over his wife's tomb. Moses was buried here, alongside his wife, in 1885.

As well as bringing Jerusalem to Ramsgate, the Montefiores also took something of Ramsgate to the Holy Land. The Mishkenot Sha'ananim almshouses they built, in one of the first Jewish neighbourhoods to be established outside the walls of the Old City, used decorative ironwork specially imported from G. S. Culver's East Kent Metalwork factory in Ramsgate.

Above: Rachel's Tomb, Jerusalem, the model for the Montefiore mausoleum in Ramsgate. (Library of Congress)

Left: The Montefiore Windmill, Jerusalem, based on the Hereson flourmill on the East Cliff estate. (Ralf Roletschek under GNU Free Documentation License 1.2)

The Mishkenot Sha'ananim almshouses, Jerusalem, feature decorative ironwork from Ramsgate. (Eldad Cohen under Creative Commons 4.0)

The landmark Montefiore windmill, constructed close by, was based on the Hereson flour mill located on the East Cliff estate. Once shipped to Jaffa, it took forty men and a fleet of camels four months to transport it to Jerusalem. Sir Moses built the mill in order to break the Arab monopoly on flour and to provide work for Jews outside the Old City walls.

The area he built in was later named the Yemin Moshe quarter in Sir Moses's honour, Yemin Moshe being a biblical allusion meaning 'the right hand of Moses'. The mill ceased functioning in the 1890s but, in 2012, with help from descendants of the company that built it, its sails revolved again.

In 1865, in what is now Montefiore woods – between the synagogue and Dumpton Park Road – Sir Moses built the Lady Montefiore Theological College, a *yeshiva* for rabbinical students. The Tudor-style red-brick building was built to replicate a theological college in Jerusalem, in a crescent with library and reading room on the ground floor, a lecture hall above, five scholars' residences on either side, plus a ritual bath house or *mikveh*. The buildings were demolished in 1961.

Of East Cliff Lodge, only the Grade II stable yard and Grade II* glass house remain.

Sir Moses's hundredth birthday, in 1883, was declared a public holiday in Ramsgate. All businesses closed and there was a banquet at the Granville Hotel. On his 101st birthday, following further celebrations, Sir Moses gave a gold chain of office, its links in the shape of the semitic letter 'mem' for Montefiore, to Ramsgate's mayor. It is still in use. Following his death on 28 July 1885, thousands lined the streets from East Cliff Lodge to the synagogue. In his will, Sir Moses left a sum of money to Pugin's parish of St Augustine.

Sir Moses Montefiore's 100th birthday celebrations, as reported in the *Illustrated London News.*

As he had died without an heir, the Montefiore estates passed to his nephew, Joseph Sebag. Queen Victoria, who had known Sir Moses since childhood, gave Sebag a knighthood and licence to use his uncle's name and coat of arms, and he became Joseph Sebag Montefiore. The Sebag Montefiore name lives on in the historian Simon Sebag Montefiore, Sir Moses's great-great nephew, and his wife Santa, the novelist.

Florry Cottages, at Nos 91–101 Hereson Road, recall a sad story related to Sir Joseph, who took over the estate. He built them, in 1888, in memory of his youngest daughter, Sarah Floretta, known as Florry. A few years before Sir Moses died, she had been staying with her great-uncle at East Cliff Lodge when she was taken ill and died suddenly, aged fourteen. The Montefiore crest appears on No. 95. These were almshouses, or model cottages, for deserving Jews and Christians.

DID YOU KNOW?

In 1838, rioting fish hawkers fought with troops brought from Canterbury, in what was called the 'bloodless battle of Harbour Street'. The recent Ramsgate Improvement Act had made it an imprisonable offence to sell fish in the street but, following a public outcry, the practice was allowed to continue.

Today, Ramsgate's Jewish community is much diminished, to the extent that in 2012 Simon Sebag Montefiore told the *Jewish Chronicle* it was 'an increasing struggle' to maintain the mausoleum in the town, where there is very little 'viable Jewish life'.

He raised the possibility that Sir Moses and Lady Judith might be reburied next to the landmark for which they are most famous in Israel, the Jerusalem windmill. He told the newspaper he had spoken to Israeli Prime Minister Benjamin Netanyahu at the ceremony to reopen the mill: 'I told him that a lot of the family thought it was about time that Sir Moses was brought back to Jerusalem.'

Sebag Montefiore told the audience at the windmill dedication: 'Moses Montefiore loved Jerusalem, lived for Jerusalem, and even made it our family motto. A Zionist before the word was invented, he believed in the sacred idea of Jewish return as a religious Jew's duty, and in Jewish statehood.'

However, there is opposition in Ramsgate, and from the Ramsgate Montefiore Heritage, which maintains the synagogue and mausoleum, to such a move. In a statement they said: 'Sir Moses wished to be buried in Ramsgate, where he built a mausoleum for his wife, who predeceased him, and subsequently for himself. Sir Moses frequently visited Palestine but never attempted to live there nor did he state he wanted to be buried there. If Sir Moses had wanted to be buried in Palestine, this presumably would have been arranged.'

7. Famous Ramsgate Residents

Mary Townley

Mary Townley (1753–1839) was one of the first female architects. She became a pupil of the artist Sir Joshua Reynolds, and later married James Townley, who invested heavily in the construction of distinguished Ramsgate buildings designed by Mary.

Chief among them is her family home, Townley House in Chatham Street, probably the finest among Ramsgate's late Georgian and Regency buildings.

According to Historic England, 'the Townleys were the developers (and in Mary's case architect) of most of late eighteenth century, early nineteenth century Ramsgate which determines its present character [including] ... Chatham Place, Spencer Square, Royal Road, Nelson Crescent, Royal Crescent' and the Paragon. She also designed much of

Townley House, designed by Mary Townley, is architecturally one of the finest buildings in Ramsgate.

Mary Townley's family tomb in St Laurence's churchyard.

Albion Square and the mews houses behind it. In 1803 James Townley bought the park that fronts Albion Place, and in 1810 Mary acquired Albion House itself.

As Paul Nettleingham writes in *Townley House in Ramsgate*, the house, built in 1792, became a key part of elevated social life. The Townleys were one of the most prominent Ramsgate families, and held many balls and masques in the house. Among the guests were William IV and the Duchess of Kent, with her daughter, Victoria, the future queen.

However, the deaths of Mary's eldest and youngest sons, James in 1808 and Poyntz Stepney in 1810, dealt her a devastating blow. She withdrew from society, and the dazzling social occasions she once hosted were replaced with bible readings. Husband James died in 1817, by which time Mary had devoted herself to the church. Her son Henry became a clergyman.

DID YOU KNOW?
The ancient tradition of the Hooden – or Wooden – Horse, in which young people visited houses on Christmas Eve dressed in a sort of pantomime-horse costume, survived in Ramsgate until the early nineteenth century. They would be accompanied by a group ringing hand bells and singing carols. Some accounts suggest that, originally, a real horse's head was used as part of the costume.

Mary and James are buried in a family tomb at St Laurence's Church. The Townleys' central role in the development of Ramsgate makes this grave, according to Historic England, 'arguably historically the most important tomb in St Laurence churchyard'.

Townley House, with its distinctive two-storey bow, supported on Tuscan columns projecting from its otherwise flat facade, became a girls' school, then part of the Farley's furniture store, and is now apartments.

Vincent Van Gogh

Vincent Van Gogh came to Ramsgate in 1876, aged twenty-three, and taught – unpaid but in return for board and lodging – at William Stokes's boarding school at No. 6 Royal Road. His nearby lodgings, at No. 11 Spencer Square, overlooked the sea, and he wrote to his brother Theo: 'There is a harbour full of all kinds of ships, closed in by stone jetties running into the sea on which one can walk. And further out one sees the sea in its natural state, and that's beautiful.'

In another letter he said: 'These are really happy days, the ones I'm spending here, day after day, and yet it's a happiness and peacefulness that I don't trust entirely, though one thing can lead to another.'

Shortly afterwards, Stokes moved his school to Isleworth and Vincent followed.

Vincent Van Gogh's former lodgings in Spencer Square.

Sir William Garrow

You may not have heard the name William Garrow (1760–1840), but you will certainly have heard the phrase he coined: 'Presumed innocent until proven guilty.'

Garrow was a revolutionary figure who lived at Pegwell Cottage – actually a very grand marine villa – on the cliffs above Pegwell Bay and now called Pegwell Lodge.

By insisting that those who accused defendants, and their evidence, must be thoroughly tested in court he helped establish cross-examination and the adversarial court system used all over the world today.

Up until the 1730s, prisoners charged with robbery and other felonies could not have defence lawyers, despite often facing death if convicted. These were the days before an effective police force, and the government often paid large sums in blood money to bounty hunters if they could secure a conviction against a targeted individual. As a result, perjury was widespread.

Aware of this, judges began allowing barristers to defend the accused, but it was not until 1783 that Garrow appeared at the Old Bailey and transformed the situation. In ten years he defended in almost a thousand trials, almost single-handedly developing the art of cross-examination as he exposed the lies of bounty hunters. He also helped develop vital rules of criminal evidence, including those against hearsay and involuntary confessions.

Geoffrey Robertson QC, in the forward to *Sir William Garrow,* writes: 'Why was Garrow such a different class of counsel? Unlike his better-connected rivals, this young barrister of humble birth was prepared to mix with and to understand the demi-monde of coiners and counterfeiters, thieves and thief-takers. He was prepared to take the unheard-of step of meeting his clients in plague-infested prisons to take their instructions.'

He won the respect of the legal system and was appointed Solicitor General, then Attorney General, and later became a judge.

Criminals also respected him. John Hostettler, in *A Revolutionary for Criminal Justice,* writes that:

> On one occasion his wife, Sarah, was travelling with her granddaughter by coach from Ramsgate to London. Highwaymen stopped the coach and robbed everyone in it of all their valuables. The coach then proceeded along the road and the same highwaymen stopped the coach again. This time they gave back to Sarah Garrow all the things they had stolen from her, and the little necklace taken from the granddaughter, keeping all they had stolen from others in the coach.

William Garrow was the subject of three-season BBC TV drama *Garrow's Law,* drawing on verbatim records from his most significant cases. A blue plaque was placed on Pegwell Lodge in 2010.

The Littlers

Three siblings who created one of the greatest theatrical empires of the twentieth century were born in Ramsgate. Prince, Emile and Blanche were among the five children of Jules and Agnes Richeux, who in 1901 ran the Admiral Harvey – now replaced by The Mariners – on the corner of Harbour Parade and York Street. In 1906, Jules leased the Royal Victoria Pavilion before moving to Woolwich to run the Royal Artillery Theatre. When Jules died prematurely, Agnes married Frank Littler, and the children took his name.

Blanche, Emile and Prince got involved in theatre management from an early age and began building a theatrical empire. They produced pantomimes all over the country, for the first time casting big stars from comedy and film such as Stanley Holloway, Arthur Askey and Jessie Matthews.

By the 1930s they controlled half of all West End theatres, touring companies and provincial theatres. By 1947, Prince had taken control of the two biggest theatrical empires: Stoll and Moss. The Littlers ruled over the West End and provinces throughout the sixties, and also built up substantial interests in commercial television. They even gave Cameron Mackintosh – who in turn became one of the most powerful theatrical producers in the world – his first break, employing him as a deputy stage manager. Prince died in 1973 aged seventy-two.

Emile stayed closer to the production side, producing many serious plays including *The Iceman Cometh* as well as musicals such as *Annie Get your Gun.* He was knighted in 1974 and died, aged eighty-one, in 1985.

Blanche founded a touring company as well as helping to manage the theatre empire. She married the music hall star George Robey (known as the Prime Minister of Mirth) and became Lady Robey when he was knighted in 1954. She died in 1981.

The Mariners, site of the Admiral Harvey, home to The Littlers, the greatest theatrical family of the twentieth century. (Nick Barham)

Elizabeth Fry

The Quaker social and prison reformer Elizabeth Fry spent the last two months of her life in Ramsgate, staying at Arklow House, which stood on the corner of Victoria Road and Belle Vue Road. Her brother lived in Ramsgate and she often visited, hoping the sea air would improve her poor health.

One of her campaigns was to improve the conditions on transportation ships taking women convicts – and their children – to Australia. These ships would often stop off at Ramsgate after leaving London on the voyage to the penal settlements and, here and elsewhere, Elizabeth visited 106 transport ships and saw 12,000 convicts.

She persuaded captains to ensure that each woman and child would get food and water on the perilous journey, and distributed care packages including scraps of cloth, needles and thread so they could make quilts to sell when they arrived and would not be destitute.

She arrived for her last visit to Ramsgate on 12 August 1845 and died exactly two months later, aged sixty-five, of a stroke, surrounded by her children and grandchildren.

Ramsgate seamen flew their flags at half-mast in her honour, something that had only been done at the death of a reigning monarch.

Above: The site of Arklow House, former home to Elizabeth Fry. (Nick Barham)

Left: Elizabeth Fry, prison reformer who died in Ramsgate. (The Wellcome Collection)

Anthony Buckeridge

Anthony Buckeridge (1912–2004), who wrote the Jennings books featuring the comic exploits of a boarding-school boy, taught at St Lawrence College, College Road, after the Second World War. After success writing for radio, Buckeridge gave up teaching in 1950 and wrote *Jennings Goes To School*, the first in a series numbering twenty-two titles by 1977, at which point his publisher decided the books were outdated and stopped printing them. However, by the 1990s interest was such that two new volumes were published.

DID YOU KNOW?

John Croom Petit, known as the Hermit of Dumpton Cave, suddenly vanished in 1823. He had lived for three years in a chalk cave at the rear of the Hollicondane Tavern in College Road, and had a reputation for piety. One contemporary account of his disappearance suggested: 'He was an arrant imposter and humbug, who fled when he was found out.' However, his disappearance also coincided with publication of a book about him by Elizabeth Strutt. Could it be that the attendant publicity led him to flee?

Frank Muir

Frank Muir (1920–98) was born at his grandmother's pub, The Derby Arms, at No. 72 Margate Road. Despite his humble background he attended Chatham House Grammar School, cultivated an erudite air and sported a bow tie. Muir was a noted wit, raconteur and TV and radio performer. When he became assistant head of light entertainment at the BBC in 1960 and found the corporation was sitting on a series based on the Jennings books of fellow Ramsgatonian Anthony Buckeridge, he immediately put it into production. Muir went on to become head of entertainment at London Weekend Television, but may be best remembered for his appearances in a Cadbury's Fruit and Nut advert in which he sang 'Everyone's a fruit and nut case'.

John Le Mesurier

John Le Mesurier (1912–83), the actor best known as Sergeant Wilson in *Dad's Army*, spent his last years at No. 8 London Road. He suffered a haemorrhage in 1983 and was taken to Ramsgate Hospital where, after telling his third wife, Joan, 'It's all been rather lovely', he slipped into a coma and died.

He was cremated and his ashes buried at St George the Martyr, Church Hill. In 1991 Kim, one of two sons John had with second wife, Hattie Jacques, died of a heroin overdose in Barcelona, Spain, and his ashes were buried alongside him.

St George's Church, where comic actor John Le Mesurier is buried.

John Le Mesurier's remains lie together with those of his son, Kim. (Nick Barham)

Bibliography

All About Ramsgate and Broadstairs (London: W. Kent & Co., 1864 and Ramsgate: Michael's Bookshop, 2007)

Anon, *Life of St Mildred* (London: R. Washbourne, 1884)

Beckett, Ian Frederick William, *The Amateur Military Tradition, 1558–1945* (Manchester: Manchester University Press, 1991)

Caesar, Julius, *The Gallic War* (http://penelope.uchicago.edu/Thayer/e/roman/texts/caesar/gallic_war/home.html)

Castle, Ian, *Zeppelin Raids, Gothas and 'Giants': Britain's First Blitz 1914–1918* (http://www.iancastlezeppelin.co.uk/19-mar-1916/4590506241)

Catford, Nick, *The Ramsgate Tunnels* (Ramsgate: Michael's Bookshop, 2005)

Catholic Encyclopedi (New York: Encyclopedia Press, 1913)

Clarke, William M., *The Secret Life of Wilkie Collins* (Stroud: Allan Sutton, 1996)

Clayson, Alan, *Wish You Were Here: Coleridge's Holidays at Ramsgate 1819–1833* (Ramsgate: A. & C. Clayson, 2001)

Fitzpatrick, Andrew, *How Our Discovery of Julius Ceasar's First Landing Point In Britain Could Change* History (https://theconversation.com/how-our-discovery-of-julius-caesars-first-landing-point-in-britain-could-change-history-88267)

Gattie, G. B., *Memorials of the Goodwin Sands and Their Surroundings, Legendary and Historical* (London: J. J. Keliher, 1904)

Gilmore, John, *Storm Warriors; or, Lifeboat Work on the Goodwin Sands* (London: Macmillan, 1875)

Grant, Elizabeth, *Memoirs of a Highland Lady* (London: Canongate Classics, 2006)

Green, Abigail, *Moses Montefiori: Jewish Liberator, Imperial Hero* (Massachusetts: Harvard University Press, 2010)

Grehan, John, *Dunkirk: Nine Days That Saved an Army* (London: Frontline, 2018)

Healey, Edna, *Emma Darwin: The Wife of an Inspirational Genius* (London: Headline, 2002)

Hill, Rosemary, *God's Architect: Pugin and the Building of Romantic Britain* (London: Allen Lane, 2001)

Hill, Rosemary, *Pugin and Ramsgate* (Ramsgate: The Pugin Society, 1999)

Hostettler, John, *A Revolutionary for Criminal Justice* (https://garrowsociety.org/2010/02/11/a-revolutionary-for-criminal-justice/)

Huddlestone, John, *400 Facts and Curiosities of Ramsgate* (Ramsgate: Thanet Publicity Service, 1937, reprint Ramsgate: Michael's Bookshop, 2006)

Kadish, Sharman, *Jewish Heritage in England: An Architectural Guide* (London: English Heritage, 2006)

Kelly, Benedict, *The Granville Hotel, Ramsgate – Revisited* (Ramsgate: Michael's Bookshop, 2013)

Kidd, William, *The Picturesque Pocket Companion to Margate, Ramsgate, Broadstairs and Parts Adjacent: The Essential Guide for Travellers by Steamboat from the Metropolis* (Ramsgate: Michael's Bookshop, 2005)

LeGear, Rod, *Underground Thanet* (Birchington: Trust for Thanet Archaeology, 2012)

Lives of the First World War (https://livesofthefirstworldwar.org/)

McCranie, Kevin D., *Admiral Lord Keith and the Naval War Against Napoleon* (Gainesville: University Press of Florida, 2006)

Moses, Henry, *Picturesque Views of Ramsgate* (Ramsgate: Michael's Bookshop, 2006)

Nettleingham, Paul, *Townley House in Ramsgate* (http://www.michaelsbookshop.com/blogpicts2/townley.htm)

Prue, Terry, *Another World: How Napoleon Changed Ramsgate* (www.ramsgate-society.org.uk/)

Prue, Terry, *King George IV, Power Politics and Ramsgate* (http://www.ramsgate-society.org.uk/)

Richardson, Christopher Thomas, *Fragments of the History of Ville and Liberty of Ramsgate* (Ramsgate: Richardson, 1885)

Robinson, Geoffrey, forward to *Sir William Garrow: His Life, Times and Fight for Justice* (Hook: Waterside Press, 2011)

Rose, Denis, *A Ramsgate Boy's Memories of the Second World War* (Ramsgate: Michael's Bookshop, 2011)

Simmonds, Bob, *Weather Here, Wish You Were Lovely! A History of Holidaying in Ramsgate* (Ramsgate: Michael's Bookshop, 2006)

Simson, A. H., *Ramsgate during the Great War 1914–18* (Ramsgate: Michael's Bookshop, 2004)

Smeaton, John, *An Historical Report on Ramsgate Harbour* (Ramsgate: Michael's Bookshop, 2006)

Sutcliffe, Robert K., *British Expeditionary Warfare and the Defeat of Napoleon, 1793–1815* (London: Boydell Press, 2016)

The Civil Engineer and Architects' Journal (London: Groombridge & Sons, 1845)

The Littlers (http://www.its-behind-you.com/implittlers.html)

Walcott, Mackenzie, *Coast of Kent* (London: Edward Stanford, 1859)

Worsley, Lucy, *Queen Victoria: Daughter, Wife, Mother, Widow* (London: Hodder & Stoughton, 2018)

Acknowledgements

The author and publishers would like to thank the following people/organisations for permission to use copyright material in this book: The Wellcome Collection for numerous images from its archive; Peter Murphy for an illustration of his modern icon of St Mildred; Royal Museums Greenwich; Imperial War Museum; Metropolitan Museum of Art; National Portrait Gallery; Landmark Trust; and Alamy.

Every attempt has been made to seek permission for copyright material used in this book. However, if we have inadvertently used copyright material without permission/acknowledgement we apologise and will make the necessary correction at the first opportunity.